<u>BUYING USED IS OKAY - And It's a Great Deal!</u>

DISCOVER AN UNTAPPED MARKETPLACE! Near new cars in perfect condition can be bought at below half the cost of their brand new counterparts!

EXPLOIT THE CAR SALESMAN'S GREED! Every day, buyers trade in their cars to new car dealers -- for thousands of dollars below their true value. This creates a golden opportunity for <u>you!</u>

USE KNOWLEDGE AS A WEAPON! You know the dealers practically ripped off the former owner. So offer them a small profit and drive off in a great car for thousands of dollars less!

STOP POURING MONEY DOWN THE DRAIN! Learn to control an expense that bleeds most families to financial death.

DRIVE FOR FREE! Drive a quality car for two years and sell it at the same price. You bought low and re-sold high -- at fair market price. Your transportation costs! Only insurance, gas, and registration fees, for two years!

USED CARS

...How to Buy One

Darrell Parrish

Illustrations by Richard Chan

BOOK EXPRESS
Publisher

P.O. Box 1249
Bellflower, California 90706
(310) 867-3723

CONTENTS

FIND AND BUY A USED CAR -- FOR LESS!

Chapter 1 - YOU CAN BEAT THE HOUSE 1
A typical car buying couple makes a raw deal at a local car dealership. The deal is stopped by a documentary film-maker and his assistant-writer spying inside an adjacent selling-room. A savvy car-buying couple is described, and their unique car-buying strategies are outlined for us.

Chapter 2 - USED CARS -- DEALS GALORE! 27
We meet Joan and Andy Smith. They make a strong case for buying used cars, and show us exactly why. Quality used cars retain their equity, better, in their third, fourth, fifth, and sixth years of "aging." They show us how to locate the "cream puffs" on the used-car lot.

Chapter 3 - KNOWLEDGE IS BARGAINING POWER 47
Joan and Andy tell how to pre-select quality used-cars from the library. Joan calculates which used cars are more reliable and hold their re-sell values the longest of time. Andy reveals his "secret" cue-card system to show us how to determine our buying ranges from dealers' pricing data..

Chapter 4 - SHOPPING FOR A USED CAR 73
We see Joan and Andy's shopping-rules for locating quality used cars. The Smiths find several used cars and test drive them. The pre-selected car information is placed on special cue-cards, for later

use. We get to watch them "work" several salesmen, as they make their final used-car choices.9

Chapter 5 - The "Practice" Run 93
Joan and Andy return to several car lots with used cars of interest to them. They test drive an alternate used car to "test" drive the salesman, first. If the salesmen, passes their test, they switch cars and begin negotiations. If he fails, they leave for their next used-car choice. They show us how and why it's important to "practice" on salesmen and their deal making.

Chapter 6 - IN THE SELLING-ROOM, AGAIN................117
We pick up the Smiths action, as they "switch over" to their pre-selected car. The Smith's make their opening-offer and start the negotiations, again. The salesmen begins the Smiths paperwork, anew, and trys to"shuffle" them, a second time over. In the meantime, the Smiths continue "flowing" with the salesmen in their verbal-game playing. Then Andy carefully exposes his cue-card system for all to see. Nervousness besets in the manager's "War Room," over the Smith's special paperwork. Management looks worried over the time spent, while Andy and Joan "work" the tenitative "deal" in the favor.

Chapter 7 - IN THE CLOSING ROOM 147
The Smiths and the tenitative "deal" are transferred to another room and salesman -- we witness the "dirty" tricks and plans of the General inside the "War Room," as he attempts to change the Smith's deal to his favor. The General becomes "steaming" mad, as Andy refuses to release control, and then closes the deal in their favor. Mr. D, the "Closer's"

boss, is sent to save the General's deal. The Smiths quickly finish-off Mr. D, and receive a standing ovation for their victory over these infamous car salesmen.

Chapter 8 - THE CAR-BUYER'S WORKSHOP................165
"Walks" readers through Andy's cue-card system, so they can compete with car salesman and their sales managers. Summarize all necessary and helpful data for readers to prepare for a successful encounter with car salesmen.

Chapter 9 - RADIO INTERVIEW WITH Q&A 199
Typical radio interview with the author, Darrell Parrish. Some Q & A from upset car salesmen are revealed. Author has been interviewed on 1,000 or more radio and television shows, since 1981.

Chapter 10 - CORRECTIVE ACTION ON BAD DEALS 207
National organization, Consumer Credit Counseling Service release ten client-histories of car-deals that went bad, and their corrective-action to resolve these "situations" in the favor of the consumer.

Appendix A - PAYMENTS CALCULATORS 249

Appendix B - NSPECTING YOUR PURCHASE. 251

Appendix C - GETTING YOUR CAR READY FOR SALE 269

ACKNOWLEDGMENTS

I thank the following people who helped make this book possible, some inspirational, some who provided valuable information and guidance, and some who provided their essential technical expertise. I'm greatly indebted to my "editor with the glue" Mr. Philip Reed, and his wife, Vivian, for their ability to help me achieve my heart's deepest desire -- to prepare car buyers to win against the infamous "enemy," the car salesman. To Mr. Richard L. Chan's artful hand, for making my text more enjoyable. To Mr. To Mr. Paul Yates for his expert creation of the book's cue-card graphics. And, finally, to the many students who unknowingly let me to test my ideas and concepts, on them, in colleges around Los Angeles. And special thanks to California State University at Long Beach for authorizing my original materials for classroom-credit with their student population.

Darrell Parrish

PUBLISHER'S NOTE

This is a "how to" book that uses fictional characters and places to illustrate its information and themes. It is not the intention of this book to slander anyone or any profession. The book's goal is simply to teach unprepared buyers a strategy, so they can get a fair deal when buying a used car. Hopefully, readers will receive the knowledge they need to return to the "good old days" of car buying, when it was a simpler, easier and more profitable process for the public.

The author stresses readers should not take this material lightly and that only *diligent readers benefit the most from its contents.* However, after several readings of USED CARS, and with repeated applications of its cue-card system, readers should accomplish simplifying the basic process of all negotiations and benefit economically in the marketplace. It's an honor to publish Mr. Darrell Parrish, three titles on car-buying and leasing, and we sincerely hope it will restore balance in the marketplace and allow the winning attitude to prevail for all!

AUTHOR'S NOTE

After the publication of my first book, THE CAR BUYER'S ART, many readers reported they saved thousands of dollars buying new cars. After the book was on the market ten years, one thing always bothered me! How could I help the 30 millions of people who bought *used* cars, every year? While thinking of an answer to this question, I became aware of an additional benefit. Not only could I help used car buyers, but I could tell the public about a unique opportunity that has always existed. Thousands of *additional* dollars can be saved by buying a used car from a new-car lot. Used Cars..How To buy One, explains why buying used cars makes better sense. I still believe, buying quality-used cars is the best way to go. When you study my book, closely, I think you will agree, too!

After presenting my views over radio and television, these many years, I discovered a special group of people. These people buy and sell cars on a regular basis, year in and year out. To anyone wishing to do the same, I recommend Mr. Don Massey's USED CAR GOLD MINE (See Back of book for his ad). He advocates buying and re-selling to private parties, and I don't disagree with his master-plan. His book is full of tips and information about the used-car business, and advocates buying and selling used-cars as a sideline job. If you consider doing this kind of work, the money earned goes into *your* pocket -- not big business'. I hope you enjoy reading this book, and have fun putting both our "systems" into action. Happy reading, shopping, buying, re-selling, and driving!

Darrell Parrish

This book is dedicated to my father, who told me that you only need to ask, to receive. Here's how he taught me to ask!

1
YOU CAN BEAT THE HOUSE

Ann and Steve McNally are in their fourth hour of negotiations for a three-year-old Honda at a new-car dealer. As they sit, together, in the salesman's office and with their eyes glassy and palms sweaty, the McNallys wonder why they are there! Actually, they should be at the theater watching an exciting movie, together. The McNallys remembered thinking there would be plenty of time, before the show started, to take a look at an attractive Honda across the street. Unfortunately for them, they remembered little more, except of strolling across the street to ask a salesman about a price on a car!

The McNallys remembered talking with many car salesmen, during their long visit inside the dealer's office. Not even one salesman replied to their innocent question about why they were at the dealers and not at the movies. Instead, the McNallys got lots of "double-talk," a quick demo-ride in the Honda, and even faster "walking" into the dealer's office. After the McNallys entered the office, though, their car keys, trade-in's registration and cash-deposit disappeared. At one time, Mr. McNally demanded his car keys, registration papers and cash-deposit returned to him! Of course, one salesman responded to Steve's request, by sending another salesman out to search for the McNally's car keys. With all this commotion going on around and about the McNallys, the fourth salesman asked for both of them to write their initials on the paperwork in several places. One salesman asked Steve, if there were some problems with their soon-to-be-signed contract. Finally, and with such a crowd pressing in on them, now, the McNallys "felt" obliged to sign the contract. They even forgot about getting their car keys, registration papers and cash-deposit back.

Meanwhile, the dealer's sales-team continued to apply their "selling-skills" on the McNallys, until they felt accustomed to their "fate" of being sold a car, today. After all, most of the car salesmen told the McNallys, over and over, they probably got the best deal of the week! One salesman even mentioned, the sooner they sign their contract the better for them! Actually, Steve and Ann just wanted to end their ordeal, quickly. In conclusion, they do remember telling everyone of their need to own a Honda. Surely, they got that "terrific deal," everyone talked about, earlier.

One thing still bothered Steve, though. It wasn't so much the purchased price of the Honda at $14,500! It was the car dealer's $1,500 trade-in offer that bothered him the most. He really thought it was worth much more!

Let us now listen to Bob, the original salesman, and what he has to say about the McNally's trade-in.

FADE IN

BOB: As I've been saying, $1,000 is the "honest-to-goodness" best price we can give you on that Dodge, Mr. and Mrs. McNally.

STEVE: But, we paid $8,000 for it, only three years ago. It should be worth more than $1,000 to your boss, Bob! I kept the car in excellent running condition.

2

BOB:	What can I say? We can barely auction off these old cars to anyone. Used-car dealers don't want them, either.
ANN:	At work, I saw one on the bulletin board selling for $5,000.
BOB:	Now folks, you got to be kidding! At what price? Besides, selling to the public is a big hassle, anyway. Everyone knows it's very difficult to sell to the public, they complain about everything, even call up their lawyers on the littlest of complaints!

Steve turns to Ann. He believes, in front his wife, he should be much stronger. Why doesn't he know what to say or do? Why can't he counter Bob's persuasive arguments better?

STEVE:	I guess our Dodge isn't worth that much, Ann. I sure thought it was worth more, too.
ANN:	I don't know, honey. Let's go home, and over dinner think about this.
STEVE:	Ann, you're right. Bob, we want our car keys and cash-deposit returned?

Bob ignores Steve's request for his keys and even weaker attempt to walk out on him, so he continues to allure them into buying a car, today!

BOB:	Steve, you're a sharp negotiator. You've got me on the ropes, here. I know you're not going to leave such an excellent deal. I'm on your side, folks. Tell me what it will take to close this deal, today!
STEVE:	Well, if you come down on the Honda's price and come up a lot on our trade, you've got a deal with us.
BOB:	We need $3,000 down-payment, so I can present your paperwork to the manager. Will that be cash or check? I'm going to try and get you a much better price for your trade-in.

Bob throws his hands up, in a loser's gesture, and motions for two nearby salesmen to enter his office. Two salesmen approach, blocking the office's doorway in the process. Rapidly, Bob crosses out and adds figures to the McNally's paperwork. He believes his customers may change their minds and leave the office. In defense of Bob's commotion, the McNallys crane their necks to study his changes, but they can't read any of his changes very well, upside-down! Then Bob takes the down-payment check and paperwork to the sales office. He swiftly returns to the McNallys.

BOB: Okay. I the boss has approved your car loan with the bank. He has given you folks $500 more for the trade-in, and discounted the Honda another $500. Also, your interest rate on the car-loan is below bank-rates and your monthly payments are extremely low! Do we have a deal, folks?

As if to agree with Bob's "best" offer, the McNallys shrug their shoulders, and wait for the other to speak.

ANN: It's up to you, dear.
BOB: You heard her, Steve. It's your call. Yes, you both have an excellent deal, here!

Bob extends his hand -- holding a pen in it, to commit the McNallys to his paperwork! In the meantime, he rises to congratulate both of them on their excellent deal-making.

STEVE: Well I think......Okay.

Before Bob could shake hands to agree, though, a stranger barges into the office. As the stranger passes Bob's "guards" at the door, he stares at them in contempt.

DIRECTOR: Cut! Cut! Cut! It's not working at all! This is terrible!

BOB:	What is this? How dare you interfere. Who are you, anyway?
DIRECTOR:	It's so completely unbelievable for me! I can't believe salesmen can treat consumers in this manner. Who wrote this script? Get the writer in here, right now!

The McNallys are utterly perplexed having more strangers rush in on their "private" business affairs with Bob.

STEVE:	Are you another salesman?
DIRECTOR:	No. I'm the Director.
STEVE:	Director of sales?
DIRECTOR:	No! The Director of this movie. We're making a documentary movie on buying used cars. We're recording a typical deal with a hidden cameras, in the other room. But this isn't typical! It's unbelievable!
BOB:	No, it isn't. This _is_ typical.
DIRECTOR:	Why are you "robbing" these good folks of their hard-earned money, mister?
BOB:	Now, wait just a minute. We're allowed to make a profit. That's why America is really a great place to live!
DIRECTOR:	You're _taking_ profits, everywhere.

Still another person enters the crowded office, in search for his boss. He's not dressed in a suit like the other salesmen and he has a very worried look on his face.

DIRECTOR:	Who are you?
WRITER:	I'm the Writer.
DIRECTOR:	The ex-writer, unless you can justify this so-called deal to me.
BOB:	It's my deal. I "worked" the McNallys myself. I should get a full commission for my efforts.
DIRECTOR:	Stay out of this, mister! I'm talking with the my employee!
WRITER:	I can't justify it, sir. But, I can explain it.

The Truth Always Hurts

As cameramen and crew take a break, the Writer examined the salesman's paperwork. Using the *Kelley Blue Book* or *N.A.D.A Official Used Car Guide* (price guides dealers use to determine a used-car's worth, in the moment), the Writer explained why the McNallys' Dodge should be worth $3,600 wholesale, and retail for much more. In fact, the Writer mentioned "aggressive" car salesmen should get $5,000 for McNally's Dodge, easily, in its present operating condition.

Meanwhile, inside the salesman's office, Steve's face goes bright-red and dripping-sweaty, as he now realized Bob's offer was really "robbing" him of their trade's real worth.

STEVE: You mean I just about lost $3,600? How could I let this happen?

WRITER: By letting Bob convince you both, what your trade-in's worth.

STEVE:	But, how should we know what our car is worth? Bob said he knew, exactly!
WRITER:	You should have found out, ahead of time, before stepping on Bob's car lot. Really, it's your fault, folks! You two became typical impulse-buyers, as Bob "convinced" you into buying his car, today!
DIRECTOR:	What are impulse-buyers, anyway?

Now, all the car salesmen acted nervous, as they looked at one another in the tiny office. Even Bob couldn't keep quiet about impulse-buyers.

BOB:	The very best kind of customer! They are easy-to-sell folks, like the .... !
WRITER:	Bob, maybe it's easy for you. But, for Steve and Ann, and the many other car-buying folks, buying cars from salesmen is a painful event. Not all buyers are "victims" like the McNallys. Some pre-plan their entire used-car purchases, and then meet salesmen like Bob with no risk of losing their hard-earned money.
BOB:	What risk? We're the pros! All consumers need some "help" in signing their contracts. It's our policy to guide them into signing it!
STEVE:	I have to admit, we sure liked that Honda.
WRITER:	Sure you do. But there are many used Hondas out there. By locating several Hondas [same year/make/model], at different dealerships, you can select the "best" used Honda for the least dollars! Now, look --

Once again, all were bend over Bob's paperwork. Using the *Kelley Blue Book and/or N.A.D.A. Official Used Car Guide*, the Writer revealed a three-year-old Honda 4-door should be re-selling for about $12,500 to the public (the suggested retail-price posted in the used-car guide), and not the $14,500 Bob's boss wants for it!

BOB:	But we've got "tons" of overhead in our cars, and many other costs like car cleaning and waxing, safety inspections, processing fees, and much much more!
WRITER:	Well, how long have you had this Honda?
BOB:	About one week!
STEVE:	So you mean, I was about to lose $3,600 on my trade-in. Then pay Bob's boss $2,000 above the full-retail for his used-Honda -- they purchased for several thousands, below wholesale!
WRITER:	Probably thousands less. And that's not all, folks!

Ann clutches her stomach, and begins to stagger out of the salesman's office in total dismay of their situation.

ANN:	I'm going to get sick, maybe even throw up!
DIRECTOR:	So am I. I took this assignment to get away from all the violence in the movies. But, this is killing me!
BOB:	Why? Our deals are painless.

The Writer points to additional figures on Bob's paperwork, as he continues telling us all about the McNally's deal.

WRITER:	Bob's contract with the McNally's indicate they were financed through an loan company, and not a bank. If the McNallys had agreed, with their signatures, they would be paying extra-fees to the dealer -- like a broker's fee. and, here's how there "deal" looked:

Profit on dealer's used Honda	$4,500
Profit on re-sold trade-in	$3,600
Broker-Profit on financing	$ 400
Total Profit to Dealer's pocket	$8,500

Steve gazed at the Writer's bottom-line figure, then hangs his head, slowly. We should have went to the movies, Ann!

STEVE: Boy, what a sucker I was.

WRITER: Don't feel bad. You've got plenty of company. Right, Bob?

BOB: Right! I mean? We sell a ton of cars, here.

WRITER: Would you consider this a typical car deal?

BOB: Yes, this is a great deal for me. The McNallys are important to me. I'll be glad help them, in there next car purchase.

A Happy Ending.

The Director reached over and took the McNally's paperwork and contract out of Bob's hands and tore them to tiny pieces.

BOB: Hey! What are you doing? This is a "private" office. You can't stop this deal.

DIRECTOR: I'm tearing up your deal, right now!

BOB: You can't interfere! We'll call the cops.
DIRECTOR: I can do anything I want, mister. I'm the
           Director! That's why I'm tearing up this
           script, and the Writer and I are going to come
           up with a new idea.

As Bob sputters and fumes behind them. The Director puts
his arm around his Writer, and they walk out into the car
lot. Among the gleaming glass and shining chrome, they
search for a new vision, together.

WRITER: You said your films must be realistic, before
           you will let the public view them.
DIRECTOR: Yes, but Hollywood loves only happy endings.
           It's up to you to show them the way (looking
           around). Look at this example of American
           business out of control! There must be a way
           for decent folks to buy used-cars, for less!
WRITER: Actually, there is a method. Not many people
           know about it, though.

The Director leans hard against one of Bob's used-cars, and waits for his Writer's intriguing answer.

WRITER: In my research for this script, I came across a couple of experts. Their names are Mr. & Mrs. Smith. They use a card-carrying <u>system</u> to buy used-cars with.

DIRECTOR: What kind of system?

WRITER: A secret system for searching out and buying quality used-cars. They purchase only used-cars called, "cream puffs." They buy them for well below dealer-wholesale, to assure a maximum return on their equity.

DIRECTOR: Below dealer's wholesale? I want realism not fantasy, mister!

WRITER: These folks are for real, sir! They have saved all their previously-owned car records to prove it, and they have taught their secret system to thousands. If I remember right, first, their system calculates which used cars are worth owning, and what price to offer them at. Next, they locate several pre-selected used cars, but only at local new-car dealerships. Then, the Smith's select their "top" five used cars and dealer-locations. Finally, one dealer at a time, they negotiate for the lowest price possible before signing. The Smith's car-buying strategies save them more money after the deal is signed, too!

DIRECTOR: I'm listening!

WRITER: Remember, Bob, the dealer's spokesman, who just about captured the McNally's trade-in for $1,500! Well, if the dealer captured that trade-in, before they put it on their used-car lot for resell, they would adjust its price to full-retail. In the case of the McNally's trade-in, that re-adjusted price would have been $5,000. Suppose for just a minute, the Smith's system "focused-on" the McNally's Dodge as a car really worth owning! And,

12

after searching the local car dealers for one, they located the McNally's Dodge waiting on Bob's used-car lot. Obviously, the next step would be to pre-calculate or "guess" what the dealer paid for it. Say the Smith's system "guessed" the car's value to be $1,500 or $2,000. What would happen if the Smiths approached Bob with their car-lot offer of $2,000. At first, Bob and his sales manager would ignore their offer! But later on -- after spending much time with the Smiths, usually the sales manager considers their offer more seriously. Many sales managers will close "thin deals," rather then losing customers to other car dealership down the street.

DIRECTOR: That's fantastic! But wouldn't the dealer's salesmen just kick the Smiths off their lot?

WRITER: Not at all. Remember, the Smiths have a card-carring system that works for them, and car dealers need to make money and pay bills.

DIRECTOR: O K, I'll bite. How does the Smith's card-carrying system work?

WRITER: I'll explain it to you, later. But, first I need to tell you more about how car salesmen take advantage of consumers.

Your Archilles Heel on the Car-Lot

The Director ponders deeply over his thoughts, meanwhile the Writer opens his thick notebook to better explain:

1. Car salesmen have "insider" knowledge. Salesmen know what your trade-in's worth and what they can resell it for. Also, they know what was paid for their car. With this "insider" information, they can pre-calculate their profit, as the deal progresses. Car salesmen know other things, too, like how much financing can be "pushed" into the customer's deal, and which add-ons, like insurance and warranties, can better "sweeten" their profit position.

13

2. Car salesmen play at their "home-court."
All "visiting" teams to a sports event are vulnerable
when placed in unfamiliar surroundings. Consumers
entering into a buying "arena" once in three-to-five
years are in no less of an vulnerable situation. Often,
car salesmen exploit "visiting" car buyers, who
wonder into their "home-court" by taking away their
car-keys, DMV documents, and/or cash-deposits;
anything to "hold" them "hostage" while inside the
salesmen's offices. If car salesmen can keep their
customers "hostage" for a while, their sales managers
will gain valuable selling-time to persuade these
"visitors" into buying cars, today. Sometimes, sales
managers send in specially trained "players" to help
convince customers they need to sign, now!

3. Car salesmen work in groups or teams. By
training groups of car salesmen to "work" together,
the sales manager greatly increases the odds of
selling more cars to more customers for more profits.

Therefore, using sales teams to sell cars makes economical sense. In other words, when car salesmen lose "control" of their customer, they <u>must</u> release them to other "players" to assist the sales manager at selling cars. By "turning-over" customers to other salesmen, the sales manager gets another "chance" to sell cars, today. Hence, "aggressive" car salesmen never work alone, but in groups. Remember, these sales groups take their "orders" from sales managers and/or sales specialists called, closers!

4. Car salesmen use selling-plans to win. Car salesmen use selling-plans that help them "control" their car-buying clientele during the negotiations. These "selling-plans" are followed by every car salesman working for an "aggressive" sales manager. Their "plan" is divided the into three major selling zones: car-lot, selling-room and closing-room. When car salesmen are "working" their customers into signing contracts favorable to them, they "envision" themselves passing through these three selling-zones.

In other words, car salesmen imagine themselves going through three logical selling events to aid their sales managers sell more cars for more money. And when car salesmen "step" out of this selling-plan, "aggressive" sales managers discipline them.

5. **Car salesmen are experienced negotiators.** Car salesmen practice their selling-skills, everyday! Normally, when all sides understand the "rules" of competing, we all cheer for the better "player" to win! Unfortunately, most "aggressive" sales managers have "rigged" their side of the negotiating-table with -- not one player, but many players against one buyer! If that weren't bad enough, sales managers observed consumers are easily mislead or confused when at the negotiating-table, especially when more sellers enter to complicate the buyer's thinking process. If car buyers fail to grasp the salesman's complicated selling "tactics," they usually negotiate poorly at the negotiating-table. But, when buyers do comprehend the salesmen's complicating selling-plans, usually, they fair very well at the negotiating-table. Example of a sales-ploy: When car salesmen "work" customers with no-credit and/or no available cash to buy cars, by "turning-them-over" to other front-line salesmen, so they can "practice" on them. Usually, the newly hired salesmen must "practice" with these captured "lookers," until their closers or sales managers "order" the salesmen to sent them off the car lot!

The Writer rushes through his notes about car salesmen "practicing" on consumers, while the Director drops his head.

DIRECTOR: Can you go on like this all day?
WRITER: If you want me to, sir!
DIRECTOR: Please stop. I'm getting too depressed. Let's get on to the good stuff, before we lose our audience. I mean, didn't you say consumers can win at the car buying game!

WRITER: Yes, I mean exactly that!
DIRECTOR: If so, then I'm fascinated with these Smith's car-buying system. Who are these Smiths, anyway? Do they live nearby?

The Smith's Strategy

The Writer believes he has found the Director's new vision. Everyone enjoys a story about underdogs winning against wealthy business adversaries. The Smiths are definitely the underdogs, here! Of course, every dog has its day, and that's what the Smiths have been doing, over the years. Actually, Mr. Smith has been interviewed, on radio and TV, for well over sixteen years, now. Currently, he has been teaching night-classes at local junior-colleges, to assist his students increase their car-buying skills. Mr. Smith believes his consumer-advocate position with "aggressive" car-salesmen, has made a difference with his students. For he gets letters from them, explaining in detail of their buying "victories" over the infamous car salesmen.

The Writer changed his topic to the Smith's secret car-buying system. Once again, the Director scribbles in his notebook. Here's some of the main points to the Smith's car-buying system:

1. Search for cars with <u>high</u> re-sale values. By reading Consumer Reports Magazine, concerned car buyers can select quality used-cars that possess excellent resell-values. Each year, Consumer Reports magazine releases [April issue] new and used-car's articles discussing every car's merits in the market. When consumers read through the articles, carefully, they can get an "experts" opinion of which new and used cars are "valued" worth owning. The magazine's editors evaluate new and used car data, based on the car's recent make and model repair histories. With this kind of "expert" facts gathering, consumers can pre-select quality cars, based on the car's historical evidence, and not rumor.

2. Consider <u>only</u> three and four-year-old cars with high resell-values. New cars and old cars can cost their current owners lots of money. New cars cost their owners lots of money because they devaluate for the first three years, heavily. Older cars cost the owners lots of cash because of major repair bills, poor road reliability and difficulty to resell. On the other hand, buying three-to-four year old cars may give their owner's minimal loss from devaluation, better dependability on the road, and are easy to resell. Typically, cars with high resell-values are more reliable past their fourth years of "aging." And cars with low resell-values are less reliable past four years of use. Therefore, great "bargains" exist by choosing car's with high resell-values.

3. Shop at new-car dealers, only! New-car dealership's with "aggressive" sales managers often get their trade-in's at very low prices because their

sales team "steals" them from previous customers. "Aggressive" sales managers keep only the very best trade-ins for re-stocking the used-car lot. Also, they place the "best" salesmen there to re-convert their past customers' trade-in equities back into cash. This is especially true of "aggressive" car dealers who capture over 45% of their total dealer-profits off used-car sales. Remember, trade-ins kept for resell, doesn't yield the sales manager any cash, until one of their salesman resells them to used-car buyers. For this reason alone, sales managers prefer to resell their recent trade-ins, fast, so they can recoup the hidden-profits back into cash. Finally, to get at this "hidden-cash," sales managers usually discount these trades to "aggressive" buyers who know how to ask.

4. If new-car dealers re-condition their used cars, go elsewhere. Informed car-buyers look for used-cars with extra TLC (Tender Loving Care) still in them. Quality used-cars with lots of TLC in them are cars worth owning. Quality used-cars with lots of TLC in them "age" better over time! And, when informed car-buyers locate quality-used cars with lots of TLC and low-mileage, too, they seriously consider them as cars worth shopping for. On the other hand, when a car dealer's service department cleans and paints their car's motor [detailing motor] it becomes impossible to verify how much TLC was given by the car's original owner. Furthermore, if car dealer reconditions the trade-in's with scented-perfumes it becomes impossible to determine if the car's been treated right in the past by its previous owner.

5. Locate the best five used-car choices, on your shopping list. New-car dealerships have lots of used cars for sell, but only a few are quality-used cars with lots of LTC in them. Therefore, its very important informed-buyers try to locate only quality

used-cars with lots of TLC in them, even if it takes additional new-car dealer visitations to locate them. Also, when car-buyers visit new-car dealers to locate quality-used cars with lots of TLC, they get some "exposure" to the selling "tactics" and sales "ploys" car salesmen practice. After being "exposed" to the ways of car salesmen, car-buyers get "desensitized" with their verbal chattering and paper game-playing. This "thickening" of the car buyer's "skin" during car shopping helps them later on, when walking-way from over-bearing salesmen is required.

6. **Shop and buy on separate days, always!** By dividing your car-buying "mission" into two major buying-steps, car shopping and car buying, the buyer can reduce their odds of becoming an impulse-buyer. Most unprepared car buyers break this simple rule, though, and become easy "prey" to car salesmen over-eager to sell them any car, today! When you shop and buy on separate days, though, it's very difficult for car salesmen to excite you into making a financial decision in the moment! Remember, buying the wrong used-car at any price is a serious financial mistake.

7. **Learn how to consume the car salesmen's valuable selling-time.** "Practicing" what to say and do in front of car salesmen makes good sense. The only way to "practice" with salesmen is to meet them where they work. Since car salesmen only work at car dealerships, car buyers must go meet and "practice" with them there. Why not! Most coaches instruct their team players to practice before the game! Negotiating for a used-car is no different. It's a contest of wits between buyers and sellers. Savvy-buyers believe car salesmen are "fair-game" to practice on. And the most important lesson to learn, while practicing with car salesmen, is to be able to "talk" with them in a time-consuming manner. Car salesmen consider their selling-time with a customer limited and valuable, so why not learn how to consume it -- your way!

8. Make your car-lot offer and then "walk" the salesman to his office. Car salesmen get surprised when customers take "control" away from them during negotiations. Typically, salesmen take "control" of their buyers, before trying to present them with cars and deals. When savvy-buyers locate their quality-used cars, they present their car-lot offers to their salesmen and then "walk" them to their office to begin negotiations. Likewise, car salesmen must "walk" all potential car buyers to nearby offices, so they can "focus" on selling them cars, today! Once inside, salesmen spend the rest of their allotted selling-time putting their customers on paper! For savvy-buyers though, they plan -- in the beginning hour of negotiations to "flow" along with their car salesmen in a non-competitive manner (consuming precious selling-time), until they decide its time to take "control" from the car salesmen. When the salesmen lose "control," savvy-buyers re-structure the car salesmen's impending car deals to benefit them, financially!

9. Appear confused when car salesmen try to take control of you, then change the deal with your cue-cards. Car salesmen pre-qualify their customers in the first ten or fifteen minutes of meeting. It's the salesman's job to sell all customers, and assist the sales manager in converting them to <u>today</u> buyers! When customers get qualified as non-buyers or as "lookers," by the in-experienced car salesmen working at the dealer's, they often get "dropped" by these car salesmen searching for today-buyers. Experienced car salesmen, on the other hand, are trained to "keep" their customers from "escaping" the car lot. Therefore, because it's "natural" for car salesmen to hold onto their customers the longest of time, that savvy-buyers are able to work excellent car-deals with them. Also, when savvy-buyer "act" like they are confused or confounded, car salesmen "feel" they have "control" over customers and can guide them into car-deals that favor the dealership. In other words, "acting" confused and confounded relaxes most car salesmen.

10. After the car salesmen begin his paperwork, start interfering by using your cue-cards. It takes one-hour for most car salesmen, to basically fill-in the buyer's paperwork. Salesmen divide their basic-negotiations in four-selling steps: Trade-In Price; Dealer-Car Price; Down-Payment; and Monthly-Payments. After each selling-step has been presented to the car buyer, the salesmen must pre-determine what was gained [financially], before they "recycle" them through the selling-steps, again. In other words, car salesmen negotiate with their buyers by "visiting" each of the four-selling steps. During each of these "visits," they try "taking" extra cash or trade-in equity from their clientele! Savvy-buyers, on the other hand, begin their negotiating, in the middle of the salesmen's "recycling" process. In fact, they prefer car salesmen "recycle" them as many times as they wish for consuming their selling-time.

Also, during the salesman's "re-cycle" of car buyers, savvy-buyers have more time to study their cue-cards and prepare "better" defense strategies against car salesmen.

11. Offer your trade-in as "bait," during negotiations, then take it back, later on. A great way to consume salesmen's valuable selling-time is to talk about your trade-in and why its worth more than the dealer's willing to pay you. By letting the salesmen think they are capturing your trade-in for well below wholesale -- "steal" it from you, savvy-buyers get to consume additional selling-time. Then, when the deal is about to get signed, the savvy-buyers change their minds and take-back the trades. Most savvy buyers know "talking" trade-in value with car salesmen consumes their vital selling-time in a non-aggressive manner. And when the time is right, they just remove their "bait"-- the trade-in, before a written contract arrives for signatures.

12. Sell your trade-in to a private party. Savvy-buyers protect their car's remaining TLC during ownership, so they can resell it to a private party for maximum profit. And, since savvy-buyers often get their quality-used cars [Q-cars] for well below dealer-wholesale, they stand excellent chances of getting near full dealer-retail, i.e., their original-investment, when they sell the car to a private party. Now, that's great news for anyone wanting to reduce their total cash-outlay on car ownership, maintenance, and operational expenses.

Finally, the Writer finishes with his written out summary, the Director looked amazed and even pleased with his note-taking skills!

DIRECTOR: You make it sound so easy.
WRITER: With a little role-playing skill and self-preparation you can win, too!

DIRECTOR:	Anyone can do it?
WRITER:	Yes. Anyone can win, providing they are willing to spend a few hours preparing!
DIRECTOR:	How can we teach the public to win, easily? I mean watching a film is one thing, competing in a salesman's "hot box" is another....
WRITER:	Maybe, if we set it up, realistically, people can "experience" their car-buying situation, before going in for real.

The Director's eyes widen, as he began to envision all the possibilities of releasing a consumer-education film to the general public. It would be good for the country. He could be famous. Even win awards!

DIRECTOR:	We can transcribe recorded dialog inside the salesman's office. For concerned consumers, we can copy certain acting-parts from the salesmen's dialog, so they can "practice" their acting parts from the film's scribe, and maybe even improve their buying skills. Are the Smiths trained specialists?
WRITER:	No, but as I said earlier, they truly believe in the idea "practice makes perfect."
DIRECTOR:	I love it! Let's go meet the Smiths.

2
USED CARS -- GALORE!

Andy Smith smiled broadly at both the Director and the Writer, standing at his front door. The Writer finished explaining to Andy, how he and the Director got involved in writing a documentary on car buying. Andy, then shook both their hands and invited them inside his house to continue discussing about car buying. Here's what they said:

ANDY: You've come to the right place. Come on in.
DIRECTOR: Do you mind telling us your car-buying system?
ANDY: No. Not at all!
WRITER: Maybe you can teach us, your way, to buying used-cars. Will you help us?
ANDY: Of course, I will help.
JOAN: Actually, it's difficult to get Andy to stop taking about buying cars.

Meanwhile, Joan joins her husband to invite Andy's guests to make themselves comfortable in their living room. After coffee was served, Andy's guests get down to business. The Director opened the discussion with a nagging question.

Why Buy Used?

DIRECTOR: Why not buy new-cars, instead, with your secret car-buying plan?

ANDY: Veteran car salesmen will tell you the big money isn't selling new-cars, but in selling used cars to the public. "Aggressive" sales managers get most of their used-car stock from previous new-car buyers. They capture trade-ins, for well below their "fair" market values, to resell them for huge profit gains. And at the same time, "aggressive" sales managers must buy and sell their new-car stock, but at manufacturer's pre-determined prices to the general public."Aggressive" sales managers "enjoy" taking big profits from potential customers, and selling used-cars gives them huge profit possibilities. Anyway, our "system" pre-determines which cars -- new or used are worth owning and which ones aren't. What savvy-buyers soon discover our car-buying system identify certain quality used-cars that "act" just like having money in the bank.

JOAN: We search for certain three-year old used-cars with extremely high-resale values, and tons of "tender-loving care" in them!

WRITER: Joan, you sound a lot like a ex-car salesman!

JOAN: You have to think like car salesmen, to beat them at their own game.

Andy wanted to give his two guests additional historical background vital to the future movie-script's development. The public has never "trusted" the car-selling profession, and only after the mid-1950's did "aggressive" sales staffs surface in new car-dealer showrooms to take "control" over all car salesmen and develop into profit-taking machines!

The Good Old Days of Car Buying:

Andy told The Writer and Director his father was a car salesman in the late '40's, '50's and '60's, that car buying was much simpler back then. In those days, car-buyers stayed focused on the purchase price of their cars and trucks they were considering to buy. If the car salesmen refused the buyer's car-lot offers, they would just leave and do their business, elsewhere. Also, during this time period, fewer car-dealers financed their cars. Typically, financing of cars was undertaken by special-loan companies and/or banks located near the car dealerships.

By the mid-60's, though, the financing of cars became more common place at new-car dealerships. During this time period, consumers were exchanging their late model cars about every third year. Many new-car dealers made extra-money through their new and used-car sales departments, and in-house financing flourished, too. New and used car dealers were spring up in most of the larger cities. It was great times, for everyone. Typically, car-buying population exchanged cars when their car-loans had expired. And when they did trade in their cars, they got new ones for more monthly payments. New-car dealers were happy because little down-payment cash was needed to get customers into new cars. Customers were happy because they could drive new cars every three years. New car sales sky-rocketed! Everyone was happy with their newly found prosperity. Andy's father, in the past, could get most families into new cars without "stealing" their children's lunch money. All that changed by the mid-70's and on.

The New Days of Car Buying:

By the time the mid-70's had arrived, Andy's father decided to leave the car-selling business for retirement. During the mid-70's, 80's and 90's, major economic changes occurred and reversed this country's car-buying habits, forever. To get new-car sales out of its depressionary-slump, car manufacturers gave cash-rebates and free new-car options' packages to their buyers who bought their slower selling cars. In the years that followed, new-car sales and profit margins increased. Meanwhile, new-car dealers discovered how to benefit from the inflationary trends in the nation's economy. Many of the "aggressive" new-car dealers inflated their new car's retail prices, even higher, so they could "take" more dealer-profits for themselves. Soon afterward, many new-car dealers placed their own price tags [dealer stickers] on new cars, so they could get their "fair share" of the consumer pie, while the inflationary trend continued to affect the country. As most of the "aggressive" new-car dealerships flourished, further, they bought more new-car dealerships in their area and nearby cities. During this expansion of "aggressive" car dealers, many of the better sales managers left their employment to "work" in their own -- in new-car dealer franchises of their own. Many of these "aggressive" new-car owners, taught their sale teams the selling-secrets needed to "take" extra profits from unwary car buyers.

By the mid-90's new-car buying had slowed down, mainly because few families could pre-qualify for their new-car no cash-down and/or extended-loan automobile purchases. Meanwhile, new cars were getting very expensive to buy, outright! Even, new-car trade-ins yielded little or no cash to their previous owners when returned to the dealers. Since, fewer new-car buyers were capable of buying "entire cars" with their current credit ratings, leasing become their only alternative to "drive" new cars, again. To make leasing attractive, though, auto manufacturers and new-car dealers had to spend millions of advertising-dollars to convince the public leasing was really okay. But for many, leasing wasn't okay, nor was it any "cure" to their new-car-buying woes. By the time the 90's arrived, the average financing terms on new-car loans, extended to six and seven years. With such extended-loan terms, many new-car buyers discovered, too late, that many "make and model" cars don't last that long on the road. In fact, many consumers are still making their monthly-payments on cars no-longer running. Since, auto manufacturers must sell their new-car products, somehow, leasing became their only alternative to "push" expensive new automobiles back into the marketplace.

Leasing automobiles to the public is big business for new-car dealerships. Consumers who couldn't get financed on their new-car purchases, can easily lease even more new-car product for about the same monthly payments, as in the past. Leasing became too "easy" for many consumers. They continue leasing their cars, over the years, not realizing their economical loss -- of not owning any car's equity. Soon after, leasing became more complicated as "aggressive" sales managers realized their profit potential -- getting more up-front cash form customer yielded them additional dealership profits. Thousands of excited leasing-customers paid their up-front "new-car-delivery" fees with their credit cards. With even fewer consumers having available credit-card cash on them, car dealers continue to "recycle" their "old" new-car leasees with expensive brand new cars. Evidently, this is the "latest" means by manufacturers to "push" more product on previous new-car customers!

The leasing "game" was developed to allow new-car dealers to "recycle" their customer base, every few years, with similar makes and models new cars. If customers decide to lease more new cars from car dealers, they must return to the same dealers where their lease-contracts terminate at. In other words, when a customer's lease-contract expires, the sales manager has another "chance" to re-sell or lease them. This "re-cycling" of new-car customers is easy money, because each time customers are re-sold or leased into other new cars, sales managers can "take" more car-equity [cash] from these "recycled" customers. Then, when it comes time to resell those returned-lease cars [bought for well below wholesale, too], the sales managers can capture even more dealer-profits for the dealership he works for.

DIRECTOR:	I'm so depressed. How could this have happened to our citizens and for so many years? Where was our government?
JOAN:	Taking their profits, too!
DIRECTOR:	What do you mean!
ANDY:	Joan meant to say, everyone's on the take, these days!
WRITER:	Is this the reason you buy used cars, Andy?
ANDY:	Partially. But to help you appreciate, why buying used cars is okay, I need to explain more about a car's "true" equity.
DIRECTOR:	[Smiles] What has real estate got to do with buying cars?
ANDY:	Savvy-buyers buy their used-cars with the intention of re-selling their equity later on. A car's equity is its "true worth" on the street, as it ages through use and time. In the automobile business, a car's listed dealer-wholesale value is its "true worth," only to other dealers. In the banking business, a car's "true worth" is its listed loan-value! All these figures are available to us and documented in the *N.A.D.A. Used Car Guide* and *Kelley Blue Book*. These pricing guides are available at most public libraries. So,

when I determine a car's "true worth," it's never the dealer's wholesale prices or what banks believe the car's true worth is, but what the street "marketplace" lists it at.

Equity in a Car?

By evaluating a car's "true worth," based on its resell value or loan value, helps consumers establish economical reasons for owning the car. Since every car's loan-value is already documented, several times a year, in the *N.A.D.A. Official Used Car Guide or the Kelley Blue Book*. Therefore, anyone can establish what their car's "true worth" by simply referring to either of these reference-books. Remember, car-devaluation [depreciation] take away portions of every car's "true worth," each year. For example: In the car's first year of "life," depreciation and the dealer's new-car profit will represent a huge lose [about 20% of the car's original retail price] the very moment drive the car off the lot. Likewise, in the car's second and third years of "life," depreciation can chip away another 20% of the car's original selling-price! Because of these huge losses in a car's "true worth," most savvy-buyer's try to locate specific make and model cars that "age" retaining the highest of resell values, as possible. And, at the same time, enjoy the car's for a short time with losing too much of the car's equity in the mean time.

In other words, after researching which new-cars hold onto their resell values the longest of time, savvy-buyers locate the older models [three-year old] for possible purchase. Ideally, these savvy-buyers drive their quality-used cars for about two years, before reselling them to private parties. In fact, savvy-buyers prefer driving their Q-cars for short periods of time to avoid consuming much car-equity when the car's sold back into the marketplace. This is the savvy-buyer's way of enjoying "slightly" new cars and still protect their original investment in the car they are driving. In other words, by taking the car's invested cash out, every two years [reselling it], they avoid thrusting too much of a car's "true worth" right out its tailpipe.

DIRECTOR:	Car's with equity! Who would believe it. You mean I can get my money back?
JOAN:	By taking care of our car, we can retain most of our invested-car money at resell time.
ANDY:	By transferring the remaining TLC in our cars -- to the next owners, we get rewarded with extra cash in our pockets.
WRITER:	How come millions of people continue to buy new cars, then?

The Trap of the New Car

Buying new cars is an exciting experience for most people. After purchasing their new cars, they get to show them off, to friends, associates and family. In the recent past, typical families were purchasing about fifteen new or used cars, in their lifetimes, spending about $300,000 in the process. When you add to these fifteen purchases each car's total financing costs, operating expenses, and insurance fees, it's not difficult to realize cars are an expensive "venture" to own and drive, these days.

Sometimes, consumers try to calculate their car-costs over a lifetime, but most stop counting when their trade-in's losses are figured into the equation. Of course, the amount lost buying a new car depends on many factors: What you paid for it, what other profits did you gave the dealer, the car's financing arrangements, and the trade-in's amount given by the dealer. The truth of the matter, most new-car buyers don't determine their "loses," until after they resell them [as trade-ins] back to the dealer. And, if they try to forecast their "true" losses -- say over an entire lifetime -- they will discover their new-car habits are costing them hundreds of thousands of dollars. Obviously, for many, wanting a new car in the driveway carries a steep price tag!

WRITER: If buying new cars is a mistake, why aren't used cars a better bargain, these days?

ANDY: Frankly, there are better ways of spending your new-car buying dollars. It's not that difficult to locate and buy two/three/four year-old cars with lots of *Tender Loving Care* remaining in them. When you buy slightly-used cars, and drive them for only two years, you can nearly drive them for "free." I mean "free," only if you buy them below wholesale.

DIRECTOR: Nobody drives cars "free," except maybe the owners of car dealer's and their families.

ANDY: [Andy leaning forward] Currently, there are many ex-salesmen who buy and re-sell used cars with little or no money coming out of their pockets. They simply buy them at excellent prices, and ride them, until they are re-sold to somebody. Ex-car salesmen consider their used-car stock, "temporary transportation," and/or "rolling" cash, always ready to be converted right back into cash and a nice profit.

DIRECTOR: Is there a way to choose cars that sale easily, without becoming a car salesman, too?

JOAN: That's exactly what we asked Andy's father. He told us to make a depreciation-chart on each car we liked, before considering it for purchase.

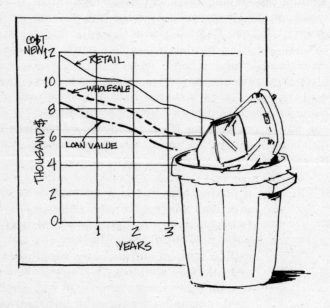

Depreciation in Cars

All car's depreciate with use and time. Also, some make and model cars depreciate worst than others. And, if cars are driven excessively, and/or are given improper maintenance, they devaluate even further. Devaluation, wear and tear, and excessive mileage, take their tow on all cars. These "impacts" change a car's "true" worth, in dollars, and are documented in two reference-books to provide the auto-industry, car dealers, and other auto-auction's personnel a "common ground of reference" for evaluating any car's worth, as time goes on. Both reference books, *N.A.D.A. Official Used Car Guide* and *Kelley Blue Book,* have been mentioned earlier.

Typically, "average" new-cars lose one-half of their original purchase price [M.S.R.P.] within four years. Each year after, the "average" car's resell-values taper off because of more reasonable depreciation factors. Some make and model cars are exceptions, because their recorded depreciation-values are either above or below the "average" new-car norm. "Above-average" new cars lose about one-third of their original-price [M.S.R.P.] within four years of "life." Each year after that, though, their depreciation-factors drop in even amounts -- well into their older years of "life." For "below-average" new-cars, it's quite a different story. They act more like "throw-away" cars, because they lose much more than one-half of their original-price [M.S.R.P.] within their initial four years of "life." Unfortunately, for the future owners of "throw-away" cars, their resell values continue to plunge right into the "trash can." These cars are difficult to resell when they are "slightly" new and impossible to resell when they are "slightly" used.

Before leaving this topic, lets take a good look at an "above-average" new-car's depreciation-chart. Try to determine a dollar-for-dollar appreciation of why "above-average" cars are worth owning for today's savvy-buyers (See Figure 1).

Quality-Used Car's Depreciation Chart
Sedan 4Dr

"age"	Retail	Wholesale	Loan Value	Deprec.
new	$	$	$	$
1	$14,200	$11,900	$10,800	$2,300
2	$12,000	$10,100	$ 9,000	$1,800
3	$ 8,000	$ 7.100	$ 6,300	$3,000
4	$ 7,500	$ 6,000	$ 5,400	$1,100
5	$ 6,400	$ 4,850	$ 4,300	$1,150
6	$ 5,700	$ 4,200	$ 3,600	$ 600
7	$ 4,500	$ 3,500	$ 2,800	$ 700

Figure 2.1

In the above example, the car's yearly-depreciation drops greatly in its first three years of "life." Then the car's yearly-depreciation begins to level off, during its fourth to seventh years of "aging." Remember, all new-cars devaluate in their initial three years of use, heavily, because new-car dealers take their profits, too, while the car's depreciating. After the third year passes, most "above average" new-cars continue to drop in depreciation, but in even dollar-amounts, each year after. Savvy-buyers consider these cars worth owning. In other words, savvy-buyers consider a car worth owning when its depreciation-factors drop in similar dollar-amounts during their ownership. Typically, this period for "above average" cars is during their third to fifth years of use. And, when the savvy-buyer purchases their "above average" car, not at its three-year old value [dealer-wholesale price], but at its five-year old dealer-wholesale price, they get to drive the car for little or no money out of their pockets, except for car and reapirs, if any! More on this topic, later.

Joan and Andy are seating together, as the Writer and Director listen to their discussion on car-buying.

JOAN: Now, you can see why buying cars -- slightly "new," makes lots of sense. Before we sell them, we use two years of the car's equity.

WRITER: If you consume a car's, how do you get to drive for free?.

ANDY: First, we don't consume the TLC in our cars. Second, we buy our cars well below dealer-wholesale -- the same dollar-amount the car depreciates two years into the future.

DIRECTOR: I understand now! You buy the car so cheap, when it comes time to resell it you sell -- higher than what you paid for it.

ANDY: That's true! Also, if you choose an "average" or "below average" car, depreciation is too extreme for you to recover your "investment."

JOAN: We only buy quality three-year old cars with high re-sale values, and lots of TLC in them.

In our opinion, there are only three types of used cars available in the marketplace, today!

"Throw-Aways," Q-Cars and "Cream Puffs:"

Throw-Away Cars. A car is called a "throw-away" when it's yearly loss -- due to depreciation, fails to slow down during its third, fourth, and fifth years of "life." In other words, some make and model car's devaluate throughout their entire "life-cycle," heavily! Likewise, these cars are difficult to resell to both dealers and private parties, at any price, and at any "age."

Quality Cars. Any car that devaluates evenly during its fourth, fifth, six, and seventh years of "life." Some Q-cars are capable of retaining excellent re-sell values, even when they pass their tenth year of use. These cars are easy to resell to both dealers and private parties. There are lots of quality-used cars [Q-cars] available at new-car dealerships, but savvy-buyers look for only the "best of the best" used cars to invest their hard-earned used-car dollars in.

Cream puffs. Any quality used-car that has been "babied" by its previous owner with low mileage on its odometer. In other words, the car still looks brand new and loaded with much "curb-side appeal." Savvy-buyers like to own and resell "cream-puffs," because they are easy to sell to private parties at a premium. Also, there are few, if any, major repairs needed by the second owners [savvy-buyers], during the two-year running of the Q-car. *Caution: Don't say to car salesmen "Do you have any cream puffs," they may think you are a car salesman "spying" on them!*

DIRECTOR: That makes sense. How do you expect to buy "cream puffs" from new-car dealers for well below wholesale? I don't think it can be done.

ANDY: Sure it can. It takes learning some car buying "rules" and "practice" on a few car salesmen.

JOAN:	If you believe car dealer's typically "steal" their used-car inventory -- from previous owners, why can't we "steal" them back!
WRITER:	What stolen cars are you talking about?
ANDY:	Stolen in the sense car dealer's took-in trade-ins [from previous new-car buyers] at well below their wholesale values.
JOAN:	Usually, we <u>search</u> and <u>buy</u> our quality used cars from "aggressive" new car dealerships. Typically, their sales managers sell -- for less, when put to the test. If these dealers have taken in a "cream puff," Andy will spot it. If the car has lots of of TLC in it, we'll make a car-lot offer on it. Of course, our specialty is making car salesmen, slip up, and we do that often enough, during negotiations.

Andy hands a handout to the Director and Writer for review. Here are some of the more important points listed on Andy's handout:

<u>Borrowing Cars</u>. It's smart to buy used-cars of quality, especially if the cars have lots of TLC in them. Typically, quality used-cars experience fewer repairs, and "age" much better then "throw-away" cars. Savvy-buyers try to locate and buy only the "best" quality-used cars in their area. They focus on "above" average three years old Q-cars, that still look and drive like brand new cars. Typically, these cars have less than 30,000 miles on them. "Borrowing" Q-cars with much TLC in them, give savvy-buyer's means of cheap transportation. When savvy-buyers buy and resell Q-cars [cream puffs] over the years they are able to maintain their original used-car investments. This is especially true if buyers get their Q-cars for well below dealer-wholesale.

<u>Never buy from Used-Car lots!</u> Avoid used-car lots, entirely. The main reason is used-car dealers pay too much for their cars. This is especially true, if they buy from new-car dealers, and/or at local auto-auctions. To buy a quality

car -- near its loan-value, would be impossible from used-car dealers. Also, it's too dangerous to buy cars at used-car lots, because you may be buying a "lemon" in disguise or even a "clipped" car -- two cars [their better halves] welded together. Don't waste your valuable searching or buying-time, and don't even "practice" on their salesmen! Just stay away.

<u>**Used Car Bargains at New-Car Dealerships:**</u> Some new-car dealers only re-sell the used-car stock near their retail prices. These non-aggressive dealers owner's don't require huge profits-margins from their sales managers. In other words, the dealer's owner is very patient with their sales department and manager. Unfortunately, these new-car dealerships usually don't discount their used cars enough to interest savvy-buyers. Sales managers who work for non-aggressive dealer would prefer to "safeguard" their in-stack inventory and salesmen's selling-time, then to sell used-car "cream puffs" at huge discounts to a bunch of bargain hunters!

Remember, bargains exist, for the savvy-buyers, because the "aggressive" a sales manager's first "rule" is to sell cars, and sell them, fast! Their second "rule" is to not count their profits, until after the contract is signed by the customer! In other words, selling cars is serious business to "aggressive" sales managers and their owners. In fact, any "rule" that maximizes their "profit-taking" ability or car-sales turn-over are worthy rules to enforce on their car salesmen!

Two Kinds of New-Car Dealers:

The Straight Sell House. Some new-car dealer's are traditional in their selling methods, and demand less profit "taking" from their sales departments. Typically, their car salesmen are one-on-one with their car-buying clientele. Also, they avoid confusing or confounding their customers for profit-taking reasons, and take their profits in a non-aggressive manner, always. Also, straight-sell salesmen are more patient, sometimes "sincere" with their customers and their transportation needs. Often, sales managers will give discounts on their cars, but only to their steady customers. And, if any customer gets too demanding with them over a car's selling price, the sales manager just asks them to leave the dealer's and go shopping elsewhere. Unfortunately, for the public, they shop at new-cars dealership's offering "fantastic bargains!"

The System House. Car dealers who hire sales managers that use groups of salesmen to sell their cars to the public. Often, "aggressive" sales managers use both "aggressive" advertising and selling techniques to achieve their yearly-sales quotas. Often, "aggressive" sales managers utilize selling-tactics that depend on confusing and confounding their consumer's decision-making process. To help consumer error in their car-buying decisions, "aggressive" sales managers send many salesmen -- several times, in and out the salesman's office. During each of these "visits" customer's are questioned or interfered with during the negotiating process. The salesmen's loyalties are to themselves, to their sales managers, to the selling of cars, and never to their customer's <u>real</u> wants or needs! For this reason, system-houses sell more cars. Remember, it's not so much that savvy-buyers are better negotiators, but that dealers get their used cars from previous owners at much lower prices -- well below wholesale! Likewise, the system-houses require their salesmen to work together to confuse and confound their customers, until they have signed their contracts. "Taking" profits come "natural" to the system-house sales managers. They know that most consumers are unprepared and unable to compete against them inside their selling-rooms -- similar to the Las Vegas gambling houses.

The Power of Money Can Be Awesome:

The Buyer's Edge. When savvy-buyers negotiate their deals with car salesmen used-car bargains exist. Remember, "aggressive" car salesmen can't distinguish one car from another, nor one buyer from another. In other words, they can't distinguish a "cream-puff" from a "throw-away" used-car, nor can they distinguish a savvy-buyer from a regular car shopper. The salesmen's only "real" concern is to sell cars, now! And the only way to sell cars, now, is to get customers to sign their contracts, today! To car salesmen, selling cars is their "way" of making a living. They know when working for car dealerships, selling is periodic and routine, at best. Only the better players [salesmen] stay employed! That is, only so many "real" customers will be sold cars, each day. It is the job of any successful salesman to capture as many of those "walk-in" today-buyers that cross into the dealer's lot.

When the Director and Writer had finished reviewing their student handout, they were walking out of Andy's front door. Andy continued talking with his guests, though, as they all stood in the doorway.

Andy: Thank goodness, savvy-buyers don't need to reveal their true intentions to car salesmen, until just prior of signing the contracts with the sales managers. By the time they reveal their intentions, car salesmen and their sale managers have too much time invested in the car-deal to let them "walk" off the car lot. Therefore, sales managers end up agreeing to a "thin deal" just to sell a car.

JOAN: It's fun to see them sweat, especially, when their bosses come-in screaming body murder about Andy's final deal.

WRITER: It's difficult to believe, Andy! These guys are pros. Why would they sign a contract that gave them little profits?

STRAIGHT SELL   SYSTEM HOUSE

ANDY: When customers spend time with a dealer's sales team, it costs money to have them work on the car lot.

ANDY: And, if sales managers believe a "real" buyers will leave them, without being sold, they prefer selling for less, than not at all!

JOAN: Actually, we were just getting ready to locate and buy our next used car. Care to come along with us?

DIRECTOR: Absolutely. In fact, what we'd really like to do is document the whole car-buying process with you and Andy as our lead-actors. Then, when you do go inside the dealer's showroom, we can get it all on film.

WRITER: [Remembering something] What about your father?

ANDY: [Andy's eyes watered] He lives in the Andes, in Chile, South America. He is spending his remaining years working a small ranch he named, "Green Mansions." He loves living there, in the mountains where no car dealers or their salesmen roam. He married a Chilean woman. He now has a wife and son to enjoy his remaining years with.

Looking Ahead:

Tomorrow, Andy will show The Writer and Director how to search for quality-used cars, and much more. In Andy's research effort, he will show us how to identify "top" quality used cars that hold on to their re-sell values the longest of time. Also, he will discuss how to fill-in his special card-carrying cue-card system, so concerned consumers can capture "top" choice used cars, for less, and enjoy their car salesmen encounters.

3
Knowledge is Bargaining Power

The Smiths greeted the Director and Writer in the reference section of the local library. Joan handed them several copies of consumer magazines to browse through. Andy selects his quality-used cars, after he reads through several articles in *Consumer Reports Magazine* and *Kiplinger's Personal Finance Magazine*. Once Andy spots several quality new-cars, he determines each car's four-year-depreciation factor from two important used-car pricing guides. Finally, after the Smiths have concluded their data gathering, they will select the "best" used-cars based on economical reasoning. Andy began his chattering, with a stack of index cards flipping through his hands:

ANDY: Choosing the "best" car with the highest re-sell value is a first priority with us.

JOAN: For us, the best car means less mechanical problems, too!

DIRECTOR: I now accept the value of pre-selecting cars, before the sale! But, why aren't car salesmen more useful to consumers?

ANDY: Knowledge is power. In the case of selling to the public, car salesmen prefer selling to uninformed-buyers. When buyers act naive or simple-minded, salesmen often put more selling "pressure" on them in the hopes of take additional profits from them. In the case of consumers, they <u>must</u> pre-determine their used-car choices or the car salesmen will choose, for them! Since, car salesmen don't sell along, but "work" customers, in groups, buying cars is more more difficult in these today's.

Consumer Reports Magazine. This magazine has a track record for delivering important and useful information about new and used-cars. Their special issues are excellent "summaries" on the automobile and truck marketplace. Inside their articles, readers are helped in pre-selecting quality-used cars. And this year's 1996 April issue is no different. It is packed with useful new and used car information for everyone to read and evaluate. In this year's issue there are three excellent reports, well worth reading: Profiles of the 1996 Cars; 1996 Cars Rating; and 1996 Cars Reliability. Please take the time necessary to review these three articles, and "fill-in" tasks, below.

In *Profiles of the 1996 Cars*, general depreciation and predicted-reliability estimates are released to readers on all new cars in the marketplace. Of course, buying used-cars is our real intention, here. However, the information in this article gives the reader a method of pre-selecting current make and model cars of value from the marketplace. From time to time, manufacturer's introduce new make and model cars. these car's lack depreciation and predicted-reliability records, because they just came on the market. If car-buyers select one of these newly released cars, they will have no documentation [repair history] to base a logical buying-decision on the car. To make a fair determination, they select an "older" version of the car -- several years back and record its devaluation data. Next, car-buyers must avoid pre-selecting cars with less than five years of "aging" history behind them. Therefore, by follow this "rule" faithfully, car-buyers should avoid pre-selecting all new-car models appearing on the market, because they have no depreciation and predicted-reliability records to base a judgement on. Q-cars need four or five years on road-testing to prove they are worthly for purchase by savvy-buyers. Cars like the Honda Civic or Honda Accord, Ford Escort or Thunderbird, and Mercury Sable, have been on the market for many years, now, and they have well-documented repair and re-sell histories for us all to evaluate. Selecting any used-car with less than a well-documented repair and re-sell history is just too much of a risk for savvy-buyer's to invest their hard earned car-buying dollars in!

Used Car Price Guides. As was mentioned earlier, there are two important pricing guides used by the auto industry: *The National Automobile Dealers Association (N.A.D.A) Official Used Car Guide* and *Kelley Blue Book.* "The N.A.D.A." releases used-car pricing data to assist car dealers and auctioneers in establishing all car's: trade-in values, wholesale values, retail values, loan values, option values, mileage credits or debts, and much more. The *Kelley Blue Book*, provides similar documentation, except for loan values on used cars. Both used-car price guides are okay for pre-determining any car's depreciation and re-sell values. In fact, these car-pricing-guides are the only means savvy-buyers have for predicting a car's future depreciation.

To begin the pre-selection of quality-used cars, three short reading "tasks" are needed to identify which used-cars are worth purchasing. We selected from the Consumer Reports Magazine [1996 April issue] three baseline articles listed below:

Task 1: From the *Profiles of the 1996 Cars* article, and after reviewing its depreciation and reliability data, select five make and model cars with the highest marks. Be sure to stay within your economical means, and then document your car-choice's depreciation and predicted-reliability values, including each car's new-car price ranges, below.

Make & Model	Depreciation	Reliability	Price Range
1.			
2.			
3.			
4.			
5.			

Next, in the Consumers Report's *1996 Cars Ratings* article, recent makes and models cars are re-evaluated and re-tested, based on each car's past test by professional drivers. These test scores are based on performance, comfort, convenience, safety equipment, and fuel economy. The comparative charts are excellent overviews on all cars in the market. After reviewing the article, pre-select similar makes and models cars, but only with the highest of ratings.

Task 2: From the *1996 Cars Ratings* article, pre-select ten highest-rated make & model cars, that you feel are worth owning.

1.		6.	
2.		7.	
3.		8.	
4.		9.	
5.		10.	

Finally, in the 1996 *Reliability* article, late make and model cars are compared, against each other, based on their collected 1993-1995 repair-histories. Pre-select only the highest-rated make and model cars the "experts" believe are worth owning, themselves. Remember, these "experts" are choosing cars that give their owners little or no troubles, while on the road.

Task 3: In the *1996 Reliability* article, after reviewing the material, pre-select ten of the "Better Than Average" late-make & model cars, listed. Stay within the same price-range, as in the above two tasks.

1.	6.
2.	7.
3.	8.
4.	9.
5.	10.

Now, compile your three lists into one large shopping-list. After compiling your three lists, together, each car should be measured against one standard: devaluation in the resell marketplace. By comparing several cars, as they are "aging," all at once, shoppers can pre-determine which used-car values best fit their available money.

It is important the final shopping-list contain only the best used-car choices. To accomplish this we must evaluate each car's depreciation values as recorded in *The N.A.D.A. Official Used Car Guide* or The *Kelley Blue Book*. These two books have pre-determined, in dollars, the "aging-process" of all cars in the market. At any time, consumers can review these pricing-guides and locate any car's yearly devaluation rate. They can even determine which car-choices hold onto their resell-values the longest. To determine a car's four-year depreciation factor, you need to "age" it four years. Then, you can look up its pricing data in a current issue of either of the above car-price guides. Afterwhich, you only need to perform a simple math equation to determine a car's depreciation factor. For example: In 1997, we look up the 1993 make and model car listed [aged car four years] in the current issue of the *N.A.D.A. Official Used Car Guide.* Then, by dividing the car's 1993 wholesale-price by its retail-price [1993 M.S.R.P.], you can determine this car's depreciation value at "age" four years. Remember too, it's important to divide [accurately] each car's wholesale-prices by each of their respective retail-prices in the fourth year! Example # 2: A 1993 quality-used car's M.S.R.P. is $15,825 [in 1993]. And it's trade-in value [wholesale] is $9,050. By dividing this car's wholesale value [$9,050} by its M.S.R.P value [$15,825}, and finally multiplying by 100, the buyer will get the car's "true" four-year depreciation-factor in a percent. Therefore, this used car's [1993 car] four-year-depreciation factor is 57%. That means, in the year 1997, this quality-used car [with average wear and tear] has consumed 43% of its original retail price within four years. And, when this quality-used car owner decides to re-sell -- to private party -- he/she should get about 57% of their original money back, minus inflation. Obviously, this car is worth owning -- but only for a short while!

ANDY: Reading these articles in Consumer Reports may seem time consuming to you, but these reading tasks are "vital" buying-steps for locating quality-used cars in the market. Pre-selecting quality-used cars based on their depreciation values makes good sense to me. Only the least-depreciating cars are worth my hard-earned money, mister.

DIRECTOR: I choose only popular cars, Andy.

ANDY: Sometimes, popular cars mean "best" cars! Popular is too vague a term, for me, salesmen use this word in their selling pitches, often!

JOAN:	We prefer buying used-cars with proven track records. I want my car's cash-value to remain in the car for the longest time.
WRITER:	If a car devaluates more than 50%, is the car still worth buying?
ANDY:	If your bank account devaluated more than 50% over four years, wouldn't you be upset?
JOAN:	After we choose our "top" used-cars, we chart each car's yearly devaluation from the *N.A.D.A. Used Car Guide or Kelley Blue Book.* We chart them, so we can predict their future re-sell prices while we own them. Since, we buy three-year-old cars, and drive them for two years, we must verify the pre-selected car's "real" worth, well into the future. For 1997, we will select only the "best" 1994 used car for our needs. But, first we must transfer our collected data on a cue-card called, shopping-cue card (See Figure 3.1).

```
+--------------------------------------------------------------+
|  LOCATION                              K >                    |
|  (Salesman's name_____ )                 |
+--------------------------------------------------------------+
|  CAR B >                    DEALER'S PRICE E >                |
|  Make/ Model/ Year                                           |
|                             Dealer's List F >                |
|                              (wholesale)                     |
|  Mileage C >              +----------------------------+      |
|                           |  G > low book              |      |
|  Options D >              |  H > high book             |      |
|     air                   +----------------------------+      |
|     leather                 YOUR BUYING-RANGE                 |
|     CD Player, etc          I >         TO          < J      |
+--------------------------------------------------------------+
```

LOCATION/PHYSICAL CUE CARD

FIGURE 3.1

Kiplinger's Personal Finance Magazine is another importance consumer magazine. The magazine's December issue is always packed with new and used car articles that can help concerned consumers in their selection of quality used-cars. Essentially, all the above mentioned tasks with the Consumer Reports Magazine can be accomplished in the Kiplinger's Personal Finance Magazine. Both magazines release "excellent" information and opinions on which car's are worth owning. Their information is both helpful and specific enough to make accurate choices on quality used-cars.

An Alternate Method to Consumer Magazines. Some savvy-buyers by-pass the magazine "tasks" and just look through their Sunday Classified Ads for a general "feel" of the marketplace, before making their minds on which of used-cars to select. One reason for searching through these consumer magazines is to expose readers to the editor's "experts" and staff. The real danger of reading new-car ads, is their ads may convert the reader into a new-car buyer! This is exactly why Andy avoids reading new-car ads, and why he hopes concerned car buyers will review the less intimidating media of consumer magazines.

Used-Car Resell-Values Can Change. As important as the above consumer magazines are, only the auto-industry's pricing-guides accurately document what car's are worth in the market. These pricing-guides "record" all make and model car's wholesale and retail values for all to see. For car dealers, these pricing guides are essential to making a profit. Even so, some used cars lose their "favor" in the auto auctions and marketplace. For one reason or another, dealers can't resell them nor can the current owners of these cars. When cars become hard to sell, dealers buy them "back-of-book" [well below wholesale] and try to sell them for a profit. Usually, these cars are poor performers, "dogs," or have troubling repair histories. Such cars are rarely recommended by the consumer magazine's auto-experts. Another good reason for doing research on your car-choices, before making an offer to buy it at the car dealers.

Trd-In	BODY TYPE	Model No.	M.S.R.P.	Wgt.	Loan	Retail
1994 TAURUS-AT-PS-AC-FWD-Continued						
125	Add Stereo Tape (Std. SHO)				125	125
250	Add Compact Disc Player				250	250
225	Add JBL Stereo System				225	225
600	Add Power Sunroof				600	600
125	Add Power Door Locks (Std. LX, SHO)				125	125
175	Add Power Windows (Std. LX, SHO)				175	175
175	Add Power Seat (Std. LX, SHO)				175	175
175	Add Cruise Control (Std. SHO)				175	175
225	Add Custom Wheels/Covers				225	225
300	Add Leather Seats				300	300
200	Add Third Seat S/W				200	200
350	Add 3.8L V6 Engine (Std. LX S/W)				350	350
475	Add Anti-Lock Brakes (Std. SHO)				475	475
400	Add Anti-Theft/Recovery System				400	400
650	Deduct W/out Automatic Trans.				650	650
775	Deduct W/out Air Conditioning				775	775
1994 CROWN VICTORIA-AT-PS-AC					**Start Sept. 1993**	
CROWN VICTORIA-V8	Veh. Ident.:( )FA( )P(Model)( )( )R( )100001 Up.					
15350	Sedan 4D	73	$19300	3786	13825	17950
16250	Sedan 4D LX	74	20715	3786	14625	18900
150	Add Stereo Tape				150	150
300	Add Compact Disc Player				300	300
250	Add JBL Stereo System				250	250
150	Add Power Door Locks				150	150
200	Add Power Seat (Std. LX)				200	200
200	Add Cruise Control				200	200
250	Add Custom Wheels/Covers				250	250
350	Add Leather Seats				350	350
475	Add Anti-Lock Brakes				475	475
400	Add Anti-Theft/Recovery System				400	400
250	Add Car Phone				250	250
1994 THUNDERBIRD-AT-PS-AC					**Start Oct. 1993**	
THUNDERBIRD-V6	Veh. Ident.:( )FA( )P(Model)( )( )R( )100001 Up.					

D O M E S T I C C A R S

Making a depreciation chart from the N.A.D.A Official Used Car Guide's data is easy to do. Lets take a look at a typical page of pricing information from a past N.A.D.A. Official Used Car Guide (See Figure 3.2).

WRITER: I like your system Andy, but I'm lousy with numbers. Charting depreciation values from reference books seems difficult to do.

ANDY: It's easy to do. Lets take time out and do a few depreciation charts to show you how easy it really is. Suppose, your car-choice is between a specific "quality" make and model car or a popular non-quality car.

JOAN: Here, Andy, I have two such examples in our original stack of cue cards.

Joan flipped through her stack of cue cards and found the pre-selected information she needed. Andy usually writes each of the car's depreciation-data on the back side of their respective location/physical-cue cards (See Figure 3.3).

Non-Quality Car's Depreciation Chart
Sedan 4-dr. (loaded)

"Age"	Retail	Wholesale	Loan Value	Deprec.
0	$16,000 (*)			
1	$14,500	$12,100	$10,900	$ (1)
2	$12,575	$10,425	$ 9,400	$2,175
3	$ 9,175 (5)	$7,325 (2)	$ 6,600 (3)	$3,100
4	$ 7,400	$5,700	$ 5,150	$1,625
5	$ 6,225 (4)	$4,650	$ 4,200	$1,050
6	$ 4,925	$3,500	$ 3,150	$1,150

Note (*)   Estimated price of car when new
Note (1). This figure would include dealer profit and the first year of depreciation on the new car.
Note (2). My highest offer on the car at three years of "age"
Note (3). My lowest offer on the car at three years of "age"
Note (4). The highest re-sell amount for the car, after I use it for two years.
Note (5). The dealer 's retail price on the new car

Figure 3.3

Of course, many non-quality cars depreciate worst then the above example has, in figure 3.3. Anyway, consumers who have completed the car-choice's depreciation-charts, using approximate pricing data, need not worry about their result. In other words, consumers can make good decisions, when to buy and resell their used-car choices, using this charting method. By studying the data on their depreciation-chart, collectively, consumers can pick the "best" year to buy the car, and in what year to resell their "best" car back into the marketplace.

ANDY: The above drafted depreciation chart reveals the correct time to buy this used car is in its fourth year of "aging."

WRITER:	Does the chart indicate when to un-load the car?
ANDY:	Yes! The best time to sell this car is in its sixth year of "aging." Owning this car three-years longer, though, may prove too costly. Even driving this car two years could prove difficult to resell, later on.
WRITER:	After reviewing this charting method, I can see the car's yearly losses in equity vary by a lot.
ANDY:	Now you're talking! After charting a few cars, you too can become keenly aware of which cars hold resell-values and which cars don't. If car buyers would only chart out their selected cars before buying them, they would alter their car-buying habits, forever! At least they wouldn't pre-selecting quality used cars that depreciate slowly over time. Or avoid pre-selecting any "throwaway" new or used cars in the marketplace.
DIRECTOR:	There are so many cars to choose from. How can I be sure of choosing only the "best" car?
ANDY:	There are many make and model quality used cars to select from. You only need to do your homework. Quality cars are not only trouble free on the road, but yield extra high trade-in dollars when re-sold to private parties. What you don't want to do is select your car, blindly. Buying used cars is risky business. Your invested money in the used-car [equity] is at risk when you select the wrong car. So, buying used-cars blindly doesn't make any economical sense to anyone! Even a well selected Q-car can give you troubles, if the car's not checked out by a reliable mechanic, first. It's important you plan out your entire car buying strategy, before ever entering a car dealer's territory! These guys aren't playing for the fun of it!

Quality-used cars perform better in the resell market, than non-quality used-cars do. The main differences with the two types are the number of years savvy-buyers can drive them and the resell-values differences at trade-in time. In other words, say the savvy-buyer wanted to keep the car more than two years, before reselling it. He/she could extend the drive time with the car with little risk of losing the car's originally-invested dollars. Here is a typical example of a quality car "aging" in the marketplace (See Figure 3.4).

Quality Car's Depreciation Chart
Sedan 4-dr. (loaded)

"Age"	Retail	Wholesale	Loan Value	Deprec.
0	$16,000 (*)			
1	$14,200	$11,975	$10,800	$ (1)
2	$12,025	$10,000	$ 9,000	$1,970
3	$ 8,775 (5)	$ 7,025 (2)	$ 6,400 (3)	$3,000
4	$ 7550	$ 6,000	$ 5,400	$1,025
5	$ 6,375 (4)	$ 4,800	$ 4,300	$1,200
6	$ 5,750	$ 4,100	$ 3,900	$ 700
7	$ 4,450	$ 3,150	$ 2,800	$ 950

Notes (*)   Estimated price of car when new
Notes (1). This figure would include dealer profit and the first year of depreciation on the new car
Note (2). My highest offer on the car at three years of "age"
Note (3). My lowest offer on the car at three years of "age"
Note (4). The highest re-sell amount for the car, after I use it for two years.
Note (5)   The dealer's retail price on the new car

Figure 3.4

Of course, not all quality used cars depreciate in the same manner as the above example has done [in figure 3.4]. When selecting a car-choice, it's important you safeguard your used-car's invested-dollars while driving it a few year more. Improper research on your purchased car may prove costly, especially if your car drops like a rock the two years you own! Your chance of recovering your invested-car buying cash would be greatly reduced. This is why savvy-buyers pre-select cars that evenly devaluate for extended periods.

DIRECTOR: I never thought about cars that way. I just go out and buy a newspaper, and then I go out buy it.

ANDY: Now do you see why your car-buying habits may be causing you money losses. In fact, buying non-quality-used cars makes no more sense then buying new cars does! And, when these cars are re-sold back into the market, they are two good examples of car-buying habits gone wrong.

As important as depreciation charts are, understanding a dealer's "true" motives and selling-plans at making profits is paramount. Also, knowing how car dealers and their car salesmen's do business, in advance, can be a great advantage to car buyers! In fact, car buyers must prepare their own counter-plans, if they really want to win against "aggressive" car salesmen working in the marketplace. To beat the salesmen at their own game, car buyers must first prepare their car-buying plans!

Cue Cards Beat the Salesman's Shell Game. It is a habit of car salesmen to be vague, in speech and on paper, while in front of their customers. The reason is simple. Car salesmen who chatter away -- in a non-committal manner to their customers, allow other "players" [salesmen] more chances to "take" profit and/or sign them to contracts. The Smith's cue-card system slows down or stops salesmen from

chattering -- talking vaguely, and/or remain non-committed on paper to customers. In other words, cue-cards reduce the car salesmen's chattering-skills to confuse and confound customers, because the cue-cards make salesmen respond to the "holder" of the "cards," just as the car salesmen's "worksheets" help the dealer's sales managers take profit. Andy's father taught him how to use the cue-card system, so he could avoid getting confused or confounded by crafty car salesmen.

ANDY: We talked about shopping-cue cards, earlier. Shortly, I will talk about two other important cue-cards.

WRITER: Do the cue-cards act like cheat sheets? Could car salemen try to take them, away?

JOAN: Not if I can help it!

ANDY: Joan holds on to the cue-cards, while I'm "working" the car salesmen and closers.

| JOAN: | When Andy needs them, I release them to him, so he can make the necessary changes on the cue-cards. |
| WRITER: | Exactly what do the other two cue cards do? |

Both location/physical-cue card and selling-room cue card collect and store vital information on pre-selected used cars, so car buyers can make their selection and negotiate against the car salesmen. With these cue-cards, in hand, buyers can focus their attention at negotiations with car salesmen. Location/physical-cue cards record specific data, on pre-selected quality cars, whereas, the selling-room cue cards, help direct the car-buyer's negotiating efforts, while they are inside the dealer's selling-rooms (See Figure 3.5).

```
┌─────────────────────────────────────────────────────┐
│  LOCATION                          K >               │
│  (Salesman's name_____ )         │
├──────────────────────┬──────────────────────────────┤
│  CAR B >             │  DEALER'S PRICE E >           │
│  Make/ Model/ Year   │                               │
│                      │  Dealer's List F >            │
│                      │    (wholesale)                │
│                      │  ┌────────────────────────┐   │
│  Mileage C >         │  │ G > low book           │   │
│                      │  │                        │   │
│  Options D >         │  │ H > high book          │   │
│    air               │  └────────────────────────┘   │
│    leather           │     YOUR BUYING-RANGE         │
│    CD Player, etc    │    I >        TO         < J  │
└──────────────────────┴──────────────────────────────┘
```

LOCATION/PHYSICAL CUE CARD
FIGURE 3.5

Both the location/physical-cue card and selling-room cue card have lettered-arrows for placing requested data in their proper locations on the two cue-cards. Here are the detailed explanations for each lettered-arrow:

A> Location: The dealer's address where you found a pre-selected car. This is your starting point for filling-in the location/physical cue card on each selected car.

B> Car: The make/model/year of car is important data. Make sure you get this information correct. Some make and model cars have option-packages attached to their M.S.R.P.

C> Mileage: After writing in a car's mileage, then don't believe it. Rotating-back a car's odometer is common practice in the used-car market. Because dealers put even higher retail prices on their low mileage cars. There is a "natural" temptation for some dealer's to roll-back used-car stock. The dirty "deed" is done by third parties traveling, city to city, trading their dishonest-enterprise into cash. These vagabonds provide their service to anyone who will pay them up-front cash. For this reason, alone, it's important to not judge a car's "real" worth, based on low mileage!

D> Option: If the car has extras, note them down. Extras like leather seats, CD-player, and sun-roof carry added value to most make and model cars. Remember, it's important to pay the least for the car, including any option-extras [of value] that may be attached to it. If possible, try to get them for free!

E> Dealer Price: The used-car's retail price as set by the dealership. Many dealers don't reveal their used-car prices, until you spend more time with their salesmen. In many cases, a car's posted-price is much higher then the final selling-price by the time contract is signed. List the car's price as quoted by the salesman. Later on, you can change it with proper negotiating skills.

F> Dealer List: The current dealer-to-dealer price for a car, as listed in the *N.A.D.A. Official Used Car Guide* or the *Kelley Blue Book*. The wholesale-price is listed on the far-left of the page [in the N.A.D.A. book]. Note: The wholesale add-on options and mileage allowances are added on, here.

G> Low-Book: The current dealer-to-dealer wholesale price, not including any added-on options or mileage allowances, as listed in the *N.A.D.A. Official Used Car Guide* or the *Kelley Blue Book*. Often, sales managers quote extra low traded-in values to "shock" their new-car customers. Actually, sales managers are trying to buy their new-car buyer's trade-ins for as little money as possible. When these trade-in's are "bought," they will re-appear on the dealer's used-car lot in a few days.

H> High-Book: The current dealer-to-buyer price for a car, as listed in the *N.A.D.A. Official Used Car Guide* or the *Kelley Blue Book*. The retail-price is listed on the far-right of the page [in the N.A.D.A. book], without adding any retail or wholesale prices for add-on options, yet.

I> Buying-Range: The low-end of your car-lot offer, as recorded in the car-pricing guides. The G > Low-Book amount, minus 10% or 15% of that figure [or its loan value]. Example: If G > equals $15,000, then times that figure by 10% to get I > $13,200.

<J Buying-Range: The high-end of their car-lot offer, as determined by the buyers. The dealer's profit is set by savvy-buyers based on a percent of the car's price. This figure is usually between 5% and 10%. The percentage depends on what the buyer "feels" the dealer should get for taking care of the used-car. Example: If I > equals $13,200, then 10% equals about $1,320 or $1,300 even. < J equals $14,500

K> The trade-in value, as listed in the *N.A.D.A. Official Used Car Guide or Kelley Blue Book*. Includes wholesale-pricing of the car's major factory installed options, and sometimes the allowance for the car's mileage -- especially, if it has been over-driven!

L> The trade-in's wholesale value, without major options or mileage allowances being added to the final amount. If yuo plan do trade in your car, try to get the dealer's wholesales price for it, including all the car's options.

M> The buyer's pre-planned down-payment cash they will put on the dealer-car, after signing the final contract. Twenty percent of a car's actual selling-price is the suggested amount, when buyers are trying to pre-qualify for outside financing at the dealership. Banks will finance a car's loan-value, only, sometimes though, they offer no-down payment car loans to new members.

N> The monthly-payments figure on a used-car you plan to purchase. When you know your down-payment amount and approximate agreed-upon price of the dealer's car and the approximate terms of the outside-financing source, you can pre-calcuate a car's monthly-payments figure by using a monthly-payment calculator (See Appendix A, for figuring you monthly-payments).

Cue-Cards Are The Buyer's "Worksheets"

Consider each item on your cue cards as vital information useful to you and the final outcome of your negotiations. Cue-cards give car buyers extra confidence and help them stay focused at getting quality used-cars, for less! Also, by having a shopping-list and cue-cards, in hand, cars buyers tend to do much better in front of "aggressive" car salesmen. In other words, locating/selecting Q-cars from shopping-lists and handling car salesmen with cue-cards make car buying an exciting adventure for most savvy-buyers.

ANDY: It is important to understand how salesmen think, while selling their cars individually and in special selling-groups.

WRITER: Isn't selling cars difficult?

ANDY: Car salesmen are stuck with the difficult task of "painting" their illusions, in front of their customers. They must excite everyone, who cross their paths into buying, now. Once the customer are sold cars, then make them think their deals are great losses to the dealer! Now, that's hard work to me!

DIRECTOR: How do car salesmen keep employed?

JOAN: They sell must cars or risk losing their job to another more "aggressive" car salesmen!

The Dealers' Selling System. Car dealers use different selling-systems that "work" for them. Some "aggressive" sales managers prefer looking like a non-aggressive dealer when "working" customers; one salesman for one car buyer. Sometimes, non-aggressive sales managers prefer looking like one of the big guys; lots of balloons and clowns walking about the car lot. No matter what "front" they portray, their car salesmen will always try to sell their available cars: If they can't find a new car for their buyers, they will try to sell them one of their "great" cars in the used-car lot; If they can't sell them either a new or a used car, then surely a 1997's new car lease will "fix" their new-car woes.

Controlling the "front-line" car salesmen. Sales managers control their sales teams with "rules" and closers. They use closers to "help" re-enforce their car lot "rules" with the "front-line" salesmen working for the dealership. Closers are the salesmen's immediate-bosses, and they put extra "pressure" on both their salesmen and customers to "push" impending car-deals, in the dealer's favor.

Controlling customers. Car salesmen and their closers work together to sell customers' their in-stock cars. Car salesmen obey their closers, or risk loss of employment. Their primary tasks are to make "friends" with potential car buyers and then sell them cars, quickly. If the salesmen loses "control" of any customer they are with, they must "turn-them-over" to other salesmen, nearby. Note: When the original salesmen turns-over their customers, to other salesmen, they get half the second-salesman's commissions if the deal gets signed. A salesman's commission can range from 15% to 35% of the net-profit taken in the car-deal.

"Walking" customers to the selling-rooms. After car salesmen qualify their customers as potential today-buyers, they try to excite the customers with an in-stock cars before "walking" them into selling-rooms. Once inside, the salesmen will fill-out all the necessary paperwork so the closers can enter to "take" their customers "over" and continue selling them. Once closers have their customers under "control," they "work" them per their sales manager's orders. If closers fail to yield enough profits, in the time allotted them, their sales managers continue the selling-process by replacing the initial closers. This changing of closers continues, until the customers have released enough up-front cash and trade-in equity to their sales managers! The allotted selling-time to "work" customers can be four or five hours. Usually, savvy-buyers spend about three or four hours to capture their "best" deals.

The dealer's "secret" paperwork. Sales managers require teamwork from their salesmen. Each member in the team is carefully "trained" at filling-in the sales manager's paperwork -- the "worksheet," in a particular method. "Worksheets" come in lots of shapes and sizes. Some "worksheets" are simple four-sectioned pieces of paper, while other "worksheets" look like real contracts. All "worksheets" are used for the same purpose: To control both salesmen and buyers -- at the same time, and to confuse and confound car buyers into negotiating deals that favor sales managers! Typically, "worksheets" have four selling-boxes: Trade-in, Price-of Car, Down-Payment, and the Monthly Payments. Originally, they were used to keep "record" of both the salesman's progress and the buyer's comments, so sales managers could better assist the car-buyers. Today, "worksheets" are often used to maneuver customers into making several negotiating "blunders," in the favor of the sales managers. Even so, Savvy-buyers often ignore these "worksheets," until its time to counter them with their cue-cards. To effectively deal with the paper "game" car salesmen, closers and sales managers use, together, savvy-buyers must review the cue-cards, constantly (See Figure 3.6 for a typical sales manager's 4-step "worksheet").

TRADE-IN	PRICE OF DEALER-CAR
DOWN-PAYMENT	MONTHLY-PAYMENTS

FOUR-STEP WORKSHEET
FIGURE 3.6

The "Worksheet's" Four-Selling Steps:

Trade-in: The negotiation-box reserved for setting the customer's trade-in price. The selling-strategy of this "box" is to repeat, many times, very low trade-in values to "shock" the customer into believing their trade-in is "worthless" to the dealership. These low trade-in values are repeated, several times over, before the closer leaves the "box" to continue the selling-process. Once, the closer takes "control" of the front-line salesman's customer, he then continues to "shock" the customer with repeated "low trade-in value" offers, until they finally "believe" and accept the dealer's offer as the truth.

Price-of-Car: The negotiation-box reserved for setting the dealer-car's final selling price. The selling-strategy of this "box" is to provide the car salesman with many opportunities to write, on paper, several high dealer-car prices to "shock" the customer into accepting their offer.

Then, the car salesman changes his position -- acts on the buyer's behalf, to offer a series of minor discounts on the dealer-car to "shock" the customer into "believing" the dealer's car must be in great demand. This is repeated, several times, until the closer enters the salesman's office to continue the "selling" of the customer. The closer continues repeating the same "shocking" dealer-car's minor discounts to the customer, until they finally "believe in" the dealer-car's high values as the truth.

Down-Payment: The negotiation-box reserved for determining the down-payment requirements needed to take delivery of the dealer-car, now! The selling-strategy for this "box" is for the car salesman to demand extra-high amounts of cash, many times over, before releasing the customer to his closer. Once, the closer has "control" of the customer in the office, he then will continue to demand extra down-payment cash from the customer, until they "believe" in these money-demands as required to take delivery of the dealer's car, now. If no extra cash is available, the closer may even ask the customer to use their credit cards.

Monthly Payments: The negotiation-box reserved for setting the customer's monthly-payment requirements to drive the dealer's car, home. The selling-strategy for this "box" is to allow the salesman many opportunities to confuse and confound their customers by placing many figures in their heads. High monthly-payment's figures are quoted, first, to continue "shocking" the customer. Then, the car salesman offers lower monthly-payment figures to the customer, so they "believe" a discount was offer by the dealer somewhere on the "worksheet." Each time the salesman offers <u>lower</u> monthly-payments to the customer, he then asks for more down-payment cash or "takes" equity from the customer's trade-in, in exchange. Finally, when the closer does enter, to take-over the salesman's customer, he too continues the same monthly-payment "discounting" tactic, until the customer becomes totally confused or confounded and ultimately "believes" most of what the closer tells them. Savvy-buyers don't fall for such a complicated selling-strategy as talking the monthly payments "game" with car salesmen. Instead, they play along with the salesman, closer and sales manager "acting" as if they are monthly-payment buyers. This play-acting helps the car salesmen consume their valuable selling-time in a non-combative manner. When the time is right, the savvy-buyers converts back to cash-buyers before the contract is presented them for signing. Sometimes, savvy-buyers prefer returning the next day to "unwind" the sales manager's complicated car-deals, back into simple cash-for-car deals. More on this later on.

Looking Ahead:

At this point, it's only important to realize sales managers use their car salesmen, closers, and special paperwork called "worksheets" to maneuver and take their profits from wary consumers who can't compete. Just how effective salesmen and "worksheets" are when savvy-buyers enter into "aggressive" negotiations with them, will be discussed in the next three chapters.

But for now, the Writer, Director, and the Smiths have left the city-library with a shopping-list of five to ten great 1994 quality used-cars to search for in the next few days.

Tomorrow, the Smiths plan to take a stack of blank location/physical cue cards with them, and after meeting with the Writer and Director at a local new-car shopping mall, they will start the second half of their car-buying phase: Shop for quality used-cars.

4
SHOPPING FOR A USED CAR

One camera was hidden in Joan's purse. The other camera's position allowed the Director to film directly into the dealer's several selling and closing rooms, across the street. The Writer and Director sat in a comfortable mobile van facing the dealership's used-car lot. The film crew was in great position to record all car salesmen's conversations with the Smiths. Later on, Andy Smith would translate what had transpired between him and the salesmen, so the Writer could finish writing his script for the documentary film about used-car buying.

Joan and Andy Smith are ready to begin their car-shopping phase. Their goal is to locate quality-used cars listed on their shopping-cue card and then fill-in requested car-pricing data on each of their respective location/physical-cue cards. The Smiths are restricting their car search to specifics 1994 make and model cars listed on their shopping-cue card. But, before they actually begin their search and location mission, they ask us to first review a few vital "car-shopping rules." These "rules" are useful to consumer's wanting to win at their car buying adventures!

Rules for Car Shopping

1.   **Visit many new-car dealerships.** It is important to locate only the "cream puff" cars, during your searching effort. If additional visits to car dealers are needed, commit the necessary shopping time to locate several car choices in "cream puff" condition listed on their shopping-cue card. When buyers negotiate over several cars in "cream puff" condition, at a time, they can leave any particular car and dealer's deal more easily. In other words, when a buyer's negotiating efforts aren't getting anywhere, they can simply stop their negotiating with the dealer! And, once the deal is stopped, they just leave for the next dealer-location on their shopping-cue card.

2.   **Shop and buy during the week.** It is important to go shopping, when car dealers are at their slowest, in sales. The early days of the week are generally the slowest for car dealers [except for holidays]. Also during the weekdays, car dealers put their second-string salesmen on the new-car lot. In other words, the more "aggressive" car salesmen work the Fridays, Saturdays, and Sundays, of each week. Usually, savvy-buyers prefer competing with the less experienced car salesmen and closers. Most of the time, new-car salesmen are willing to spend extra time with savvy-buyers [acting as potential buyers], then with the many "lookers" who browse dealerships, everyday of the week. "Lookers" are persons who act just like regular today-buyers, while in-front of car salesmen, so they can waste their "shopping-mall time" test-driving new or used cars. "Lookers" don't need to buy any cars, but they sure enjoy "acting" like they can, in front of others. Moreover, savvy-buyers find it too difficult to negotiate their below-wholesale deals with the dealer's sales managers on the weekend. Mainly because the sales manager's salesmen are too busy [weekends] to spend that extra selling-time needed to sell savvy-buyers. Furthermore, savvy-buyers understand car salesmen sell more cars on the weekends, so they re-approach car salesmen only when it's more acceptable to discount hugely on their used-car stock to "move" their cars off the lot.

3. Locate an "Amateur" Car Salesman, First. If car buyers walk directly into the dealer's used-car department, they will encounter their best selling "pros." "Aggressive" sales managers put their "better" salesmen on the used-car lot, so they are assured to capture maximum profits off their used-car lot. Also, sales managers typically put their "amateurs" in the new-car department, so savvy-buyers usually hunt for them there. It is much easier to "work" new-car salesmen, anyway, than trying to compete with the "forked-tongue aggressive-type working in the used-car lot. Remember, new-car salesmen aren't real sellers of cars -- in the sense used-car salesmen are, but instead are more like "greeters" of customers met on the new-car lot. The real car sellers are the dealer's closers and sales managers waiting inside the sales office to spin their "web of deception" over any consumer who passes by.

4. Shop with your "new start." Once car buyers select their new-car salesmen, they need to tag along with them for a while, so they can get "exposed" to their selling ways. Stay with your salesmen for about twenty-minutes looking at various new cars on the lot, before attempting to take "control" of them. This gives the buyer ample time to see if the salesman can be maneuvered or not. If the salesmen can be maneuvered -- around the new-car lot, try to "walk" him/her around several new cars. If your car salesman is "controllable," walk him/her towards the dealer's used-car lot and see what happens, next. If your salesman goes with you -- right into the used-car lot and no other salesman approaches, the dealership's sales manager is practicing the straight-sell system to sell cars. To be assured this conclusion, look around the car-lot and count the number of car salesmen you see there. If you see few salesmen walking around the car lot, the dealership is definitely using the straight-sell system. Even so, the buyer should continue to gather the requested information on the back of their shopping-cue card, before leaving the used-car lot and dealership. Savvy-buyers look for dealers who use many car salesmen to sell. Dealerships that use many car salesmen typically use the "take-over" system to sell cars.

In other words, when new-car salesmen and their customers walk into the dealer's used-car lot to select a car, and another used-car salesmen approaches to take [turning-over] the customer away from the new-car salesmen. And, even if this happens, the customer should collect as much of their cue-card data requested on the used car-choice before leaving the lot. Be sure you include a test-drive in the car, if it has lots of TLC. Remember, avoid doing any negotiations, at this time, just gather your cue-card information and leave the car lot for the next dealer-car location on your shopping-cue card.

5. Locate Only Quality-Used Cars. When car buyers search for quality-used cars on their shopping-cue cards, they should resist all attempts by the salesmen's to change make, model and year of car-choice. Once, buyers do locate a car-choice listed on their shopping-cue card, they should take a close look at the car's resell qualities. Remember, no matter what the car salesmen say or do, always remain steadfast at locating quality-used cars with great resell-values and lots of TLC remaining in them. Remember too,

when you locate specific year/make/model used-cars with little or no TLC in them, just leave the car dealership for another one, down the road.

6. Test Drive Cars On Your Shopping-List. The shopping-cue cards are designed to guide buyers through a car dealer's used-car inventory, quickly. When buyers do locate a car-choice and then want to test drive it too, they must record additional data on a piece of paper about the dealer's car: overall condition, dealer-location, year, make, model, options, mileage, and dealer-price. After completing the test-drive, the buyer must transfer their test-drive data on the back of a location/physical cue-card. Remember too, while the car's motor is running, it's very important you lift the car's hood to search for any leaks or irregularities before ending your test drive. (See Appendix B, "Inspecting Your Purchase -- Six ways to recognize a lemon!).

7. Get the First Salesman's Card. Its important car buyers retain the business card of the initial salesman they meet at each dealer-car location. By retaining a salesman's business card, car buyers can re-enter the dealership and re-locate their salesman, easier. Also, by presenting a salesman's business card to other salesmen at the dealer, you allow the initial salesman another chance at "winning" part of the commission, if you do buy your car there. Then when you do meet a salesman for the second time, you can quickly take "control" over them while re-starting the negotiating process over, again. Meanwhile, as the new-car salesmen turn-over their customers to the more experienced counterparts [used-car salesman] they often get to "see" the professional sellers "work" their customers into signing. This method of "self-training" is the quickest and best way for newly hired new-car salesmen to "learn" the necessary selling-skills to stay employed longer. Many new-car salesmen get "fired" in the first couple months on the job, anyway. Savvy-buyers prefer to negotiate with the dealer's newly hired car salesmen, so they help the "new-starts" when possible. This "action" assists other savvy-buyers and "beginning" salesmen who want to learn how to sell!

8. <u>Never</u> Enter the Salesman's Office. It is very important to remember this "rule," while shopping for cars. Car salesmen are "pros" at persuading anyone to buy, now! Car salesmen will say and do <u>anything</u> to get car shoppers inside their selling-rooms. Once inside, they will really put the <u>pressure</u> on them! There is only one exception to this rule: The buyer may enter the salesman's office, if they are planning a "practice-run" on a few car salesmen using their cue-cards. When buyers practice with their cue-cards, they become more confident at negotiating with salesmen.

<u>Getting Started</u>

The Writer and Director are listening through the transmitter in Joan's purse, as she and Andy step out of their car. The dealer is filled with "tons" of shiny brand new cars and rows of clean used cars with various invitations on their windows, such as: "Very Clean, Low Mileage, Great Buy, and Buy Now!"

As Joan and Andy browsed around the dealer's new-cars, they were hailed by a cheerful voice. They turned to see a good looking man, late 20's, white shirt and tie, and no pinkie rings, quickly approach them. Maybe this salesman is a newly-hired employee! Just what the Smiths are looking for. As the drama unfolds, though, the Writer and Director began to focus-in on the Smith's action.

FADE IN

DIRECTOR:	Everyone Quiet! Cameras! Action!
BOB:	Hi folks! My name is Bob. Are you two in the market for a new car?
JOAN:	We're not sure if we can afford one. Right, Andy?
ANDY:	How much money does it take to buy new?
BOB:	Not much. I can get you in one of these 1997s for a few hundred a month. They are practically giving them away!
JOAN:	For free, Bob!
BOB:	No, Mrs Smith! It's just a figure of speech to get folks like you, to relax.
ANDY:	That new car looks great! Can we look inside it?
BOB:	Of course, it's going for pennies over our cost. The boss is great for giving discounts off his new cars, early in the week. Why not take a seat in it, now.

Andy and Joan sit in the new car, together. The newness is intimating for both of them. They get out to walk around the new car. Their five-year trade is looking older, by the minute.

ANDY:	Bob! We better look at some of your used cars, before we change our minds.
BOB:	Okay folks, but the boss really wants to get his customers into new cars, today!
ANDY:	No the car's too expensive for us. Can you show a cheaper version?

BOB:	Well, let me see. How about this econmical family car. It's without air, but runs great on the road. I drive one home when I get off work.
ANDY:	The car is too tiny. If we get in a wreck, I don't think we will survive the crash. What do you think Joan?
JOAN:	I think we better stick with a bigger car, Bob.
ANDY:	I think we had better look at your used-car department, instead.

Bob escorts the Smiths to the used-car department, but another salesman interferes with their progress. A second salesman approaches part-way, though, and motions for Bob to meet him. They chatter for a short moment, and then Bob returns to the Smiths with a big smile on his face.

BOB:	Folks, will you please follow me. We have a good selection of used cars. We carry the best used cars in the city! The boss demands perfect used cars for his customers. You folks taking a long lunch?
JOAN:	No. Andy doesn't need to work on Monday and I work part-time -- when I wish to.
BOB:	Really? What line of work?
JOAN:	Andy works with his computer at home four days of the week. I work on the weekend, to stay busy.
ANDY:	Bob! What year is that quality-used car, over there? How much is it going for?
BOB:	Well now, that's a beauty! It's a 1994 and it's going for $15,800.
ANDY:	Don't you guys post prices on your cars, so the public to see?
BOB:	The car's prices change every few months. It's difficult to keep up with every car's price, when the market is changing so quickly these days.
JOAN:	Maybe we should select another quality-used car, honey?

Car Salesman Qualify Customer

Car salesmen pre-qualify their "walk-ins" customers, in the first moments of meeting with them, and even during their walk around the car-lot. The more experience a car salesman has, the quicker he/she pre-quality their customers. Car dealers that hire "aggressive" sales managers to sell their cars, don't allow their salesmen the privilege of pre-qualifying *their* "walk-in" traffic! In fact, successful sales managers will demand their salesmen "turn-over" all customers -- several times -- to other salesmen, before letting them "walk" off the car lot and into the grasp of other car dealers. From time to time, "aggressive" sales managers will fire a new salesman or veteran salesman, on the spot, who don't turn-over their customers to fellow salesmen before letting them leave. Experienced sales managers know, it takes several "selling" attempts, by their salesmen, before customers can be converted into today-car buyers! In fact, "aggressive" sales managers value every one of their "walk-in" customers, because it takes thousands of advertising-dollars to get potential customers to "walk on" the dealer's car lot, each week.

Meanwhile, Bob opens all the doors of the 1994 quality-used car Andy had pointed to. He even started up the car's motor, and motioned for the Smiths to enter there next car. Bob tries to pre-qualify the Smiths, so he can determine if they are potential today-buyers or just another pair of "lookers."

BOB: This car's worth every dime. A real winner! Get in and feel it's craftsmanship, folks!
ANDY: You know, we forgot your name?
BOB: It's Robert. But my friends call me Bob.
ANDY: Bob, can I have your card. I'm just terrible with names.
BOB: Of course, here!

Joan notices Bob's has re-written his name over another salesman's name on the business card. This is good evidence Bob is a new-car salesman, after all. Be sure to save any salesmen-business cards of dealer-car locations, and staple them to their respective shopping-cue cards. Savvy-buyers use their salesmen's business cards to write additional pricing information and data, during their shopping for quality-used cars.

Walk-around the car. Next, the Smiths will walk around the car and view the general outward appearance of it. They are attempting to get a good look at the car's overall condition, including any evidence that its been in a major accident. In other words, during the shopping phase, car buyers must give their car-choices a "first" physical and brief demo-ride (For details on how to examine used cars, correctly, see Appendix B).

The car's interior and exterior appearances of a car can indicate if the car's been treated with TLC. If the car looks worn out with many scratches, discolored, or carries any off-beat odors, the car's been mistreated, during its first three years of use. Really, three-year old cars should still look and drive as new cars do! Finally, if a car's engine compartment has been cleaned, polished, or waxed, you don't need to consider this car for purchase! Leave the dealership for your next dealer-car location. That's right just forget new-car dealer's who clean up their used-cars! If new-car dealers have to "fix up" their late-model cars, they probably have something to "hide" from their customers, anyway.

Bob has been watching the Smiths, during their "walk around" of the quality-used car. He's wondering if the Smiths are a pair of "lookers"-- with no intentions of buying anything from him, or are they real honest-to-goodness today-buyers that will yield him a huge profit!

BOB: So what do you think? Pretty nice, huh?
ANDY: Well, there are a couple of items we want to
            check out, first. Can we have our mechanic
            check out the car, later on? I noticed several
            problems, during the test drive.

BOB: Sure you can! I love this car. I'll be sad to
                       lose it. I think it great car for you two. I
                       think we could let this one go for about
                       $15,000.

Joan noticed the salesman reading the quality-used car's
retail-price off a red sticker pasted on the front windshield
-- it read 040541090.

Reading Dealer Price codes

Often, car dealer's place *price-codes* on their new and used
car inventories to help salesmen make on-the-spot counter-
offers to their customers. Price-coding used cars is typical
throughout the auto industry. There are different versions,
but most decipher basicly the same way. If you see your
salesman read a price-code off a car's window, try to decode
it, yourself. Here's the most basic version.

For example: 0004054109000

For the above example: The car's year was 1994, so you look
for these two numbers to identify the car's age in the price-
code. If they read from right to left, the price of the car will
read in the same direction. There are exceptions. Sometimes,
the inner-numbers [between the car's age] are read from left
to right to confuse possible on-lookers.

For Pricing-code: 0004054109000

1. Ask the salesman what year the car is. If he/she says
   1994, look for the 9 and 4 in the car's price-code. In
   the above example, the car's year is read from right to
   the left -- 1994!
2. Now, look at all the inside numbers 05410 -- between
   the 9 and 4 in on the above example! If you read these
   numbers, from right to left -- in hundreds, the car's
   retail-price will read $14,500. If you read the number
   from left to right -- in hundreds, the car's retail-
   price will be $5,410. Since the higher number seems

more correct -- for the year and model, The $14,500 should be the dealer's asking-price. Therefore, any further decoding of used cars at this dealer's should be read in the same manner.

3. Finally, ask the salesman the price of another used-car, nearby, and try to decode the dealer's asking-price, again. *Caution: If the salesmen say $15,800, but you decode it to be $14,500, they are inflating the dealer's asking price on their own!*

Joan wrote the $14,500 asking-price of the 1994 quality-used car on Andy's selling-room cue card. Obviously, Bob's car-lot discount had failed to impress them, too. Note: Bob's logic is to offer the Smiths -- an early car-lot discount, and then "walk" them to his office! The Smiths refused to be impressed; they ignored Bob's sales-pitches and plays even through their demo-ride of the quality-used car.

ANDY: Honey! Do you want to see how it rides?
JOAN: It looks okay. Why not take a short ride in it!

The Demo Ride

Bob joined the Smiths, as they left the dealer's used-car lot to test drive the quality-used car. Andy selected an off-road street, to "experience" the car's mechanical condition. He listened to the car's motor as he accelerated it, and then stopped the car, quickly, to confirm its brakes were in great shape. Then, he turned the car's front-wheels, hard to the right and left, so he could listen for unusual noises coming from the car's under-carriage area. After ten-minutes of test driving the car, though, Andy pulled it over, and popped the hood open! He checked for leaks and drips and listened for other strange noises, too. Before Andy re-entered the driver's seat, he looked under the car for signs of rusting or suspicious welding. Finally, he walked around the running car, once again, to give it quick lookover. Once inside the car, Andy returned to the dealer's used-car lot, and they all existed the car, together.

ANDY: The car runs okay. It turns to the right and the brakes need some adjusting. There's....

BOB: It's just as I said, a great little car. Now folks $15,800 is a great offer. I hope we can get that price for you. But I need to start your paperwork, first, so the boss can help!

JOAN: I don't know Andy. Are we ready to buy this car?

Staying One Step Ahead

Andy knows car salesmen must try to "walk" them into an office -- one of their selling-rooms! If Bob fails to do this, quickly, he will need to "turn-them-over" to yet another salesman! If the next car salesman fails to "walk" them into a selling-room, they too must release the Smiths to a nearby salesman. Of course, The Smiths know Bob must be thinking about "turning-them-over" to give others an equal chance at selling them before they leave the car lot. But, Andy has his own car-buying plans to follow, now, and buying Bob's car today is not part of it! Now, they must leave gracefully for their next car location.

ANDY: Well, Bob. the quality-used car has promise. The price is rather high, though.
BOB: I can help you there. The sales manager is a personal friend of mine. I should be able to get a good price for you.
ANDY: Maybe so, but we need to go elsewhere, first.
BOB: Just a moment, folks. I have a great idea.

The "Hand-Off"

Bob senses the Smiths will not commit to buying the used car, so he motions for a nearby salesman to assist him with the Smiths. Bob "turns-over" the Smith's to another salesman walking to them. He then excuses himself and leaves in search of other customers. Of course, the Smiths know they are being "worked" by another car salesman, so the dealer's sales manager has yet another chance at selling them a car, now!

BOB:	Folks, this is my manager, Henry, he will help you, folks. I need to answer an urgent phone call.
HENRY:	Bob's a little nervous, about his phone calls. He'll be returning with us, shortly. Now, how can I help you folks into that great looking Honda? Now, where were we?
ANDY:	On our way out, Henry. If we like your quality-used car -- in comparison to three others, we'll be back to see you and Bob. Thank Bob for us. Good Bye.

FADE OUT

Andy and Joan keep on walking, though, despite the steady patter from Henry about offers, to look at different cars, or come into his office and talk about some fantastic price-discounts, and/or extra high trade-allowances for their trade-in. Finally, the Smiths get in their car and close him out, for good.

End of the Shopping-phase

Complete the Shopping-Cue Card. It is important the car-choices, on your shopping-cue card, are either dealer-located or crossed off the list, before you begin negotiating for real. When buyers shop for their car-choices, they have a good chance of locating several "cream puffs." By test-driving [several] same make and model used cars at different dealer-locations, buyers can better "evaluate" which cars have TLC in them, and which do not. Once car-buyers locate their five-to-ten best "cream puffs," they should remain "focused" at dealing on these car-choices, only. Finally, after locating several "cream puff" cars at specific dealer-locations, car buyer need to put them in an "order-of-preference"-- your very best car-choices at the top of the list.

Reviewing the results. The Smiths have located four of quality-used cars at four local auto-shopping malls. When their shopping days ended, Andy countered the total number of "visited" car-lots and car salesmen to be thirty-four. Out of the thirty-plus car dealers, Andy had located only four new-car dealers with excellent "cream puffs" in their inventories. Of the four dealer-car locations only two car salesmen where identified as newly hired employees. "Cream puffs" seem to be getting more difficult to locate at the new-car dealerships in Andy's area. To visit thirty-four dealerships and find only four cars worth buying is hard work, for anyone. But so is safeguard the car-equity and resell-value of your Q-car. Choosing the "right" car is only half the mission. Now, the Smiths must negotiate a "right" price to win in today's marketplace.

The Smiths will finish filling-out a location/physical-cue card and selling-room cue card on each of the four dealer-car "cream puffs." Andy looked in a current copy of the *N.A.D.A Official Used Car Guide* to pre-determine his car-lot offers for each of the four quality-used cars. Joan called the dealer -- where the first dealer-car is located at, and made an appointment with the initial new-car salesman -- Bob, for Tuesday at 5:00. Andy believed going in at 5:00 PM, in the early weekdays, would benefit his negotiating efforts for four reason: First, because it takes about four hours to "take" a winning-deal away from "aggressive" car salesmen. Second, by spending four-hours with the dealer's salesmen, they will want to complete the Smith's deal in order to close for the night. Third, by spending four-hours, negotiating with the Smiths, most sales managers are willing to accept a "thin" deal just to go home. Finally, sales managers prefer a sale with a "thin" profit attached to it, over a non-sale.

The Decision to Trade Cars. Andy trades his cars in, every two-years, based on each car's resell-values. Since, the Smiths have driven their three-year-old car, one year longer. Currently, they own a 1991 Q-car with low mileage and lots of TLC still remaining in it. They bought it in 1994 for $6,500 -- $200 above its loan value in the moment. Now it's 1997 and Andy calculated he will lose more of his car's originally invested cash when he sells the car back into the marketplace. If he waits longer, he will lose even more of his car's originally-invested cash.

The Smiths are ready to make their car-lot "offers" on four used-car choices at four different dealer locations. But because Andy is with the Writer and Director, additional "instruction" will be needed to help them and their future audiences understand how sales managers and their "helpers," work their car-buying clientele for profit-taking reasons. The Smiths told both the Writer and Director they prefer all car-buyers "practice" with their cue-cards, first, before going in to face the infamous car salesmen for real.

Looking Ahead:

The Director's crew gathered up their filming equipment, across the street of the dealer. But before they disconnected all their cameras, they captured on film both Henry's and Bob's worried looks as the Smiths departed their used-car lot. Fortunately, most car salesmen can't see past their "wallet" or their small world of selling to the public. They didn't noticed the camera crew's boos and hissing at them -- across the street! Nor did they see Andy and Joan chatting with the Director or Writer after leaving Bob and Henry stranded on the used-car lot. Andy looked worried, though, because he was showing such a limited "picture" of car salesmen, so he told the Writer and Director to would meet him Tuesday at 5:00 PM at Bob's dealership to film how he buys used cars, these days.

5
The Practice-Run

It is time for the "actors," Joan and Andy Smith, to hit their marks and put their car-buying system into action. The Smiths have divided their car purchase into two major steps: a practice-run on a more expensive car [new car] to determine if their salesmen are "flexible" enough, and then plan "switching" to another car -- the quality-used car they really wanted. Finally, if the Smiths don't get their below-wholesale price on the car, they will go to the next dealer-car location and try again. Andy believes "practice-runs" are a vital part of "getting-ready" to face car salesmen for real. Typically, savvy-buyers can sense if the salesmen are going to be impossible to "control" or not, during their early moments of negotiating. Once car salesmen are determined "controllable," Andy's cue-card system will further assist him at maintaining "control" over Bob's closer -- Henry and the sales manager "hiding" inside the sales office. Andy feels good about being in the used-car market, again. He thinks the "game-playing" with Henry's sales manager will be a "victory."

Meanwhile, the Director placed his tiny microphone into Joan's purse, and then checked its sound level. He sensed the Smith's confidence level was high in the moment. In fact, their entire camera crew felt the excitement and expectation of the impending performance by the Smiths. It reminded the Director of opening night at the theater. Anyway, the Writer was ready to record Andy's and Joan's every move, as they prepared for their first "practice-run." He outlined their approach in his notebook: Andy would be playing the lead-negotiator and Joan would be in her supporting role.

Before they start their "practice-run," though, Joan took time to explain her supporting-role with us. She defined her "acting" role as one of a "sidekick."

The Sidekick's role

In the old Western movie days, "sidekicks" were off-beat and unpredictable characters, always ready to bring comic relief and support to the hero in his mission to outsmart the bad guys.

In used-car buying, the "sidekick's" purpose is to frustrate, confuse, confound, even derail the bad guys -- car salesmen, while giving continual support to their lead-negotiators. Anybody can be a "sidekick." A friend, roommate, spouse or co-worker can be converted into excellent "sidekicks." It's important car buyers take their "sidekicks" with them, so they aren't alone with any car salesmen when negotiating. Often, car salesmen overwhelm their car-buying clinetele when they are along. Also, if car buyers are single, they should definitely bring others [sidekicks] with them to help throw a few "monkey-wrenches" into the salesmen's well-rehearsed sales-pitches and ploys. A "monkey-wrench" is anything, said or done, that will slow down or stop the salesman's efforts to sell the customer a car, in the moment.

The main purpose for bringing "sidekicks" along with you is to divide the salesman's attention among two, three or more people. Car salesmen tend to lose their "focus" on buyers when supportive "witnesses" are around to give a helping hand. For example: Each time "sidekicks" ask questions or make statements to them, the salesmen must take extra time to respond to the "sidekick," before continuing to "sell" their customers. In other words, each time "sidekicks" talk with car salesmen, they interrupt the salesmen's selling momentum. These interruptions provide valuable thinking-time for lead-negotiators to make counterplans. And, after the salesmen completely answer the "sidekick's" question, they must regain "control" over their customers and to re-excite them into buying a car, again. The "sidekick's" goal is to slow down or stop the salesmen's sales-pitches and selling-ploys on the lead-negotiator, so the "hero" can negotiate more effectively.

Sometimes, car salesmen can block the "sidekick's" efforts. If this happens, lead-negotiators must give support to their "sidekicks," by "reprimanding" the salesmen for getting too personal with them. Usually "sidekicks" make car salesmen very nervous, because they are "witnesses" to the bait & switch selling "tactics" used inside the dealer's selling-rooms. Finally and most importantly, if the "hero" has lost "control" over the salesmen and are about to sign a bad deal, the "sidekick's" paramount task is to "kidnap" them from the dealership's property, pronto, and before signing of the contract occurs. If a "sidekick" saves their lead-negotiator from a bad deal, they will be considered the real hero, in the eyes of a friend.

Joan is putting Andy's make-up on, while he's talking to the Director about learning a few buying-rules. These "rules" are important and need to be studied by serious car buyers.

Car-Buying Rules:

1. **Never go alone.** Its importance to have a "sidekick" tag along, always! Some buyers take several "sidekicks" with them. When the buyer uses several "sidekicks," they often bewilder their car salesmen, to the point of giving up and agreeing with their car-deal, sooner. But, make sure these "sidekicks" never join forces with the car salesmen! If this

does happen, the lead-negotiator must leave the car-lot and get another "sidekick" to help them negotiate, again.

2. Consume one-hour, before "switching" cars. When the buyer begins to negotiate for a dealer's used-car, they should "flow" along with the car salesmen's dialog for the first hour or so. This will give them ample time to pre-determine, if they can "control" their salesmen and close a deal in their favor. Furthermore, it's important car buyers "experience" part of the salesmen's paperwork, before "switching" cars and/or deciding to leave the dealership. This "exposure to a salesman's paperwork will help them later on, counter the salesman's selling plans more effectively. And, if the car salesman turns out to be too "inflexible," the buyer only needs to leave the car dealer.

3. Always, bring your cue-cards. It's the salesmen's job to make car buyers believe in them both during the negotiations and after the contract is signed. Likewise, it's buyer's task, to "look" through their salesmen's "smoke-screens" to determine what actual benefits exist in the dealer's "offers" before signing any contract. By reviewing your cue-cards, often, the buyer can easily determine their buying-position, at any moment.

4. Always, be ready to walk off the car-lot. No matter how great the deal sounds to you -- don't believe it, unless your cue-cards prove it's so. It is the job of all car salesmen to make their buyers believe them right up to the last moments of signing their contracts. Many car salesmen believe they can "control" their customers with flattery. They also believe in repeating their selling "tactics" and sales "ploys" hoping their customers will believe them. So, if your car salesman's "story" is getting too hard to believe, maybe it's time to leave. Remember too, car salesmen don't brag about their "thin" deals, nor do they flatter any savvy-buyers "winning" car-deals from them. Often, savvy-buyers will get up and/or walk around the negotiating table to impress to their salesmen they may be leaving soon.

5. Some role-playing may be required. Learning how to act in front of car salesmen is a good enough reason for doing a few "practice-runs," before actually buying a car. Car salesmen practice their verbal acting-skills on buyers, everyday. Therefore, if buyers learn a few acting-skills of their own, they may become more opposing to car salesmen. Also, by getting "exposured" to the ways of car salesmen, buyers can better decipher the salesmen's "true" motives. Collectively, car salesmen function as one person -- against the buyer. In other words, salesman #1 "offers" a large discount to get buyer into his office, sooner. Then buyer's paperwork is processed and Salesman #2 enters to explain salesman #1's car-lot "offer" is in error and that the "real" offer is such and such! Then salesman #3 enters the office to explain both previous "offers" were only tentative and that their "offer" is really such and such! finally, salesman #4 enters the office to explain their "real deal" needs to be changed, here, here, here, and here. If the buyers accept their very last "offer," they are to sign here, here, and here.

Collectively, car salesmen fail to offer their clients "truth," except after presenting them written-out contracts to sign. Why can't one car salesman "collectively" present a "last offer" to the buyer? Is it possible one person could get in trouble, legally? A very difficult moral question to answer. Have car salesmen become great persuaders at both speaking and writing, so they can be charged of crimes, individually?

After reviewing Andy's car-shopping rules, the Director and Writer feel there's more to the "art" of car buying than they ever suspected. Joan finished touching up Andy's face.

ANDY: "Sidekicks" are important. Joan is great help to me. Some dealer's send two closers, to "work" us over. If they do, Joan handles one and I the other. Teamwork is important.

WRITER: I didn't think car-buying was so complicated an affair.

JOAN: The sales managers make it complicated. They believe by complicating the selling-process, additional profit-taking is possible!

ANDY: When one understands how sales managers and salesmen work together, buyers can make effective counter-plans, easily.

DIRECTOR: Please tell us more about how sales managers "work" their salesmen and customers, at the same time.

Selling the Customer a Car

Car dealers provide several services to the general public. Typically, car dealers sell, lease and service new and used-cars to the public. To maintain a large customer-base for their service departments, though, dealers have to sell and lease plenty of cars. To sell/lease cars profitability, new-car dealers must hire sales managers and salesmen to assist them. Typically, sales managers come in two "sizes" -- aggressive and non-aggressive! Typically, non-aggressive sales managers have smaller sale-teams working for them.

These small sales-teams form into "straight-sell" houses. Aggressive-sales managers, on the other hand, hire very larger sales teams, and <u>train</u> them into "turn-over" houses.

Savvy-buyers buy their quality-used cars from "turn-over" houses for two reasons: they sell many cars, and they sell them for less. The "straight-sell" houses, on the other hand, seem content with building their customer base, more then taking huge profits. Also, they avoid giving huge discounts on their cars, because the dealer's owner is satisfied with their sales manager's selling-performance. Whereas, "turn-over" houses concentrate mainly on "taking" huge-profits from all customers. And, when persons like the Smiths enter such "turn-over" dealerships, their sales managers will heavily discount their cars to get them off the used-car lot. In other words, sales managers working in "turn-over" houses train their sales teams to sell cars, first, and then count their commissions, later.

With this "simple" picture of car dealers, completed, Andy explained the ten-selling steps sales managers and their car salesmen imagine themselves taking when selling cars to the public. By envisioning these ten-selling steps, buyers can better "picture" themselves inside the car salesmen's imaginary car-selling sequence. Once you "envision" these ten-selling steps, in your head, car buying becomes as easy as walking down a flight of stairs.

Ten Steps To Selling The Customer

1. **Car-Lot Introduction.** The first few minute's car salesmen and buyers meet, together, an introduction occurs. Car salesmen try to "hook" their buyers into a car-in stock with "aggressive" car-lot discounting and/or other benefits "temporarily-granted" to get buyer interested. These salesmen know most car shoppers are interested in looking not buying cars. The car salesmen's main job is to convert a these "shoppers" into today-buyers, before they walk off the car-lot and into the hands of other car salesmen.

2. **Pre-Qualifying & Befriending the Customer.** Car salesmen pre-determine if their customers are potential today-buyers or just "lookers," before putting them into cars for test-driving. In the meantime, car salesmen must develop a kind of relationship -- be temporary-friends with customers, before "converting" them into today-buyers. This befriending of potential customers helps salesmen maintain better "control" over their customers when the "real deal" is reveled inside the selling/closing rooms.

3. **Walking the Customer to a Selling-Room.** After they qualify their customers, car salesmen must help them select one of the dealer's cars, quickly. After the car is selected [by buyer or salesman], a quick test drive occurs to get the customers "married" to the cars selected. After the test drive, the salesman "walks" their customer to a special office -- the selling-room. Once inside this special office, the salesman continues to "control" his customer with

chatter about the customer's excellent car deal, while at the same time he's preparing the necessary paperwork.

4. Writing-up the Customer. Car salesmen must get their customers, on paper, before their closers will approach and take "control" of customers and impending deals -- continue to sell these customers in-stock cars. Credit applications are filled-in, on each customer, before any sales manager or closer can determine they can be financed new or used cars! If customer's credit-ratings are poor, closers may "switch" them to less expensive new or used cars.

5. Starting the 4-Step Worksheet. Next, car salesmen must fill-in additional paperwork on the customers -- (1) trade-in data and offer, (2) dealer-car's asking price, (3) down-payment requirements and (4) monthly-payment figures. All this information must be placed on a special "worksheet," before sales managers can pre-determine their selling-plans for taking maximum profits from the buyers. Once these 4-step "worksheets" are filled in, the salesman's boss -- the closer enters the selling-room to take over both the paperwork and customers.

6. "Turning-over" the Customer. After processing the customer's paperwork through once, the salesman must release customer to his closer -- his immediate boss. The closer continues to process the "turned-over" customer's paperwork with "shocking" news about what it ready takes to buy the dealer's car, today!

7. Closer Continues the 4-Step Worksheet on the Customer. Closers continue "shocking" their customers, on paper, by "re-cycling" them through the four steps on the worksheet: Trade-in Price, Price of Car, Down-Payment, and Monthly-Payments. The closer "re-cycles" the customer, several times, until a tentative-deal is accepted "verbally" by the customer. Finally, the closer "shakes hands" their hands and asks them to initial the papers, in several places.

8. Tentative-Deal is "re-written." Once, a closer and customer is in "agreement," the tentative-deal gets changed, again. Sometimes, the original salesman will be called in to "see" the changes being made on his agreement, so the buyer may be intimidated by his "witnessing" of it. For example: Say the initial car salesman "offered" an improved radio-system to close his part of the "deal." Later on, his closer is instructed [by sales manager] to "unwind" the salesman's "offer," and scold him in front of the customers, to further intimidate them. Of course, the buyers will be "shocked" into believing the salesman was "treated" wrong! To help their "friend" out -- they accept an inferior type radio or no radio at all, in exchange. The "con" games' salesmen play on the unwary consumer can be unlimited.

9. Customer and Tentative-Deal are Transferred. The closer "walks" the buyer and tentative-deal's paper-work to yet another office, where a Finance & Insurance Manager will convert all the paperwork into a real contract. Sometimes, the sales managers instruct their F/I managers to "re-cycle" car buyers, further, for additional profit-taking reasons. The F/I manager's secondary task is to capture more dealer-profits, before the final contract gets written out -- by interesting customers to purchase special service contracts, insurance policies and/or extended-warrantees on their impending contracts.

10. F/I Manager Converts Customer's Tentative-Deal. The F/I manager's final task is to transform the car buyer's paperwork and salesman's "worksheet" into a legal contract, so the sales manager and car buyer can sign them, together. If there are no further instructions from the sales manager, the F/I manager will write-up the customer. Finally, contract gets presented to buyer for signatures.

Joan just finished putting on Andy's make-up; when Andy finished his talk on the car salesmen's ten-selling steps. Joan mentions it is important buyers maintain some mental-pictures of where they are at, during their negotiations. Once, consumers can "picture" where they are in the salesmen's ten-selling steps, they can effectively counter any sales manager's, closer's, or salesmen's profit-taking plans. Andy believes these "selling-steps" are the sales manager's "secret" ladder to successful profit-taking.

ANDY: Always, be ready to "walk out" of any deal you make, especially if its a bad one.

WRITER: Why don't salesmen see what you're doing, and walk you off their car lot, instead?

JOAN: Sometimes, they do. But, most of the time, car salesmen are so "hungry" to sell their cars, they will put up with anything, even my husband -- Andy, to close a deal!

ANDY: It's about time to get started, honey. Do you have the cue-cards ready?

Starting the Practice-run

As the Smiths step out of their car, the Writer reviews their two-pronged buying plan: The Smiths will pretend to be interested in one car -- to start the salesman in his ten-step selling sequence. Then Joan will change her mind, in front of Andy and Bob, and select another car -- the used-car they really wanted in the first place! If the practice-run goes afoul, the Smiths will drop Bob, Henry and the sales manager, and proceed to their next dealer-car location.

Joan and Andy had their sights set on a 1994 quality-used car with 30,000 miles and lots of extras on it. It's in perfect shape and has much "curbside appeal" in it. Bob's dealer noticed that too, and hung a $15,800 price tag on it. Joan's research showed the car's wholesale price should be about $10,500, though, not counting all the extras. Andy guesses the dealer probably got it for below $10,000 -- maybe even below $9,500 from a previous new-car customer. Andy has selected this quality-used car because of its 57% four-year devaluation factor. Andy thinks he can "steal" it right back out of Bob's "hiding" sales manager's hands!

Going into Action

Joan and Andy have returned to the car-lot where their future used-car is. The Q-car had not been sold last week as Bob told them, earlier. The Smiths wandered around the new cars for a while, until Bob could get free to meet them. Bob knew the Smiths were coming, because Joan had called him for an appointment at 5:00 PM, earlier. He remembered his brief encounter with them, though, but couldn't remember which car they were interested in -- over in the used-car department. Also, he was convinced the Smiths returned to buy a car from him, today.

Going into action:

Andy and Joan "act" as today-buyers, so Bob will continue to spend extra time, even through their "practice-run," before starting the <u>real</u> negotiations with Bob's closer and the sales manager. Bob is "guessing" the Smiths will become impulsive buyers, and his commission will be a huge one.

FADE-IN:

ANDY: Honey, did we forget, anything?
JOAN: No. I have the cue-cards, pencil, calculator, and extra set of car keys for the Toyota.

Selling-Step 1: Car-lot Introduction

BOB: High folks. It's just past 5:00 PM.
ANDY: Hi Bob, we like your new BelchFire V9. How much are they going for, these days?
BOB   1997 BelchFire's go for about $25,595. A great car! Built to please! Do you folks live in the area?
JOAN: Yes, about 10-minutes from here.
BOB: I hope you don't mind, but I need to ask you a few questions.
ANDY: What kind of questions?

Selling-Step 2: Pre-qualifying & Befriending the Customer

BOB: Like where you work and bank at, and what kind of car insurance you carry, now.

JOAN: We both have good jobs, have great insurance and bank at TransFed Universal.

BOB: Thanks for answering. Most people get upset when asked such questions. It's a joy to be helping you two. Your BelchFire V9 is a great choice. If I can get $1,000 off the sticker, will you buy, today?

Author's Note: What is so special about this sales pitch? The salesman is being vague and non-committal, as he speaks with the Smiths. When Bob said "If I can get $1,000 off the sticker, will you buy, today," he remains uncommitted in the first-half of the sales pitch, while on the second-half of the statement, Bob demands the Smiths give him a firm answer -- yes , that they will buy, today! These "trick" statements are made, on purpose, by "aggressive" salesmen.

Selling-Step 3: Walking the Customer to a Office

ANDY: It's way too early to make a decision, Bob. We will need to look the car over and test drive it, first!

JOAN: I like the apple-green color, honey.

Bob rushes around the green-colored Belchfire V9 and opens all its doors, even starts-up the motor to get the Smiths to enter into dealer's new car.

BOB: Now folks, these cars sell very fast. They are in great demand, too. It may prove difficult to get my manager to agree with that $1,000.

ANDY: Well lets give it a spin on the road, honey.

JOAN: Okay. Lets do it!

The Smiths begin their test drive of the Belchfire V9 with Bob in the back seat. Of course, Bob is chattering throughout the demo-ride. Andy was surprised by Bob's cleaver request to pull over the car, so he could safety check the Smith's new car. After the test drive, thought, Bob talked to the Smiths -- not as shoppers, any more, but as today-buyers.

JOAN: The radio works okay.
ANDY: Okay, where's the air conditioning switch?
BOB: The car has everything, even special rims and wheels.
JOAN: Don't like the feel of my seat, Andy. And it smells awful here. Too much plastic smell.
BOB: Please pull-over for a minute. I need to safety check your new car.
ANDY: Okay.
BOB: Turn the lights on. Left signal, right signal, emergency signal, and your brake lights. That is fine. Now, your emergency lights.
ANDY: What else?
BOB: Nothing. Let's finish the test drive, turn here, here, here, and here.
BOB: [Entering the dealership] That's a great car choice. I tell you what, if I can get you a great trade-in allowance -- on your car, and try and get you that $1,000 discount-offer, will you buy, today?
JOAN: Can we buy it, now!
BOB: The Belchfire V9 has great value, extending beyond belief. I mean, next year, your car could be worth even more! tell you what. lets go inside and work up some figures.
ANDY: OKAY. But, only if I get a great price for my trade-in!

Author's Note: Andy didn't make any car-lot offer, here, because he doesn't carry any cue-cards on the new Belchfire V9. During the practice-run, negotiations can progress in the dealer's favor. Besides consuming value time, Andy is trying to discover if Bob, sales manger and incoming closer can be "controlled," during the practice run. If they bend a little, Andy will continue to negotiate with them -- the second time around, but for another car.

Selling-Step 4: Writing-up the Customer

BOB: Now, make yourselves comfortable, folks. Do you care for Cokes or coffee?

JOAN: A Coke will be fine, and Andy drinks coffee, black with no sugar, please.

Author's note: Some sales managers "bug" their selling-rooms with listening devices to maintain control over their sales people. Some savvy-buyers use hand signals or talk in a foreign language to keep their car salesmen guessing. It is wise thinking to restrict all private-conversations, between car buyers -- spouses or "sidekicks" while you are inside the salesman's office. If you must talk to your spouse or "sidekick," leave the selling-room, first.

BOB:	[Returning with the refreshments] I am happy for both of you. I have a credit application and other paperwork to fill out. Also, do you have your car-drivers licenses, and DMV-papers on the trade-in?
ANDY:	[Hands Bob a filled-out credit application and photocopies of their licenses] I keep a copy of this application-form to help me remember all the names, dates and numbers. This should keep you busy, Bob.

Selling-Step 5: Starting the 4-Step Worksheet

BOB:	[Short-time, later] Now, lets get down to business. The price on our car is $25,595 plus special racing rims and wheels. With the rims and wheels, your car totals $27,095 plus tax and license fees!
ANDY:	What about the discounts you promised us, earlier. That sounds like a lot for a new car.
BOB:	We sell twenty of these new BelchFire V9, each weekend.
ANDY:	Well, my 1991[Older Q-car] trade-in should bring the balance way down, anyway.

Bob starts the 4-step worksheet on the Smith's, first, by filling in the top half: Price of Car and Trade-In Allowance. Bob simply writes in the figures -- new-car's sticker price without giving the Smith's any "visible" discount. Next, to "shock" the Smiths further -- verbally and on paper, Bob announces a very low trade-in price for their trade-in. After this bit of "shocking" news, Bob quickly writes on the 4-step worksheet that very low trade-in offer. Bob, makes sure Andy and Joan both see the figures he's writing, and then assures the Smiths -- he's on their side! He even asks for their car keys, before he can catch his breathe. Finally, Bob mentions, maybe, his dealer's forthcoming appraisal may give the Smiths a much higher value on their trade-in (See Figure 5.1).

TRADE-IN	PRICE OF DEALER-CAR
$2,000 $1,000 $?	$25,595 + rims wheels $27,095 + T/L -$1,000
DOWN-PAYMENT	MONTHLY-PAYMENTS

FOUR-STEP WORKSHEET

FIGURE 5.1

BOB: I hope we can get you $3,000 for it, anyway!

JOAN: We need more than that! Our car runs great.

BOB: I hope so! But, if I can get you another $1000 off the new car, do we have a deal?

ANDY: It's way too little. Try harder, Bob.

BOB: Even if I get $1,000 off the new car, and more for you trade-in, we still need $8,000 down-payment! Our banks want 1/3 down cash.

ANDY: Why $8,000 dollars!

BOB: If your credit is good, maybe less! Let me do some figuring, first. Ah yes, your payments are about $416. Now, that's with our $1,000 new-car discount!

Bob continues "shocking" the Smiths, further, as he fills-in his 4-step worksheet. If the closer doesn't enter, soon, Bob must "re-cycle" the Smiths through the 4-step "worksheet," again. On the other hand, if Bob feels he is in complete "control" of the Smiths, the closer or sales manager may instruct him to continue "re-cycling" them, anyway, until more profits show up in the paperwork (See Figure 5.2).

TRADE-IN	PRICE OF DEALER-CAR
$2,000 $1,000 $?	$25,595 + rims wheels $27,095 + T/L -$1,000
DOWN-PAYMENT need $8,000 now	MONTHLY-PAYMENTS $416/ mo

FOUR-STEP WORKSHEET
FIGURE 5.2

ANDY: I don't know where you are getting all those numbers, but they seem extra high to me!

BOB: Which figures bother you, Andy?

ANDY: [Talks about monthly-payments to consume Bob's selling-time] Well, I don't understand why the monthly-payments are so high.

BOB: What figure would you like to see, Andy?

JOAN: $350 would be more like it!

BOB: To get your payments lower, I need cash. How much cash are you thinking about?

ANDY: $3,000 cash plus trade. I need $5,500 for it!

BOB: [Writing, swiftly] Well, let me see. $3,000 down-payment. Will that be cash or check?

JOAN: Check, of course. We don't carry that kind of cash with us.

BOB: Ah yes, a $3,000 check, right now! Here's my business card. The dealer's name is _____.

JOAN: I'll write the $3,000 check, but hold on to it, in case we don't like your deal, Bob.

BOB: I need to show my boss some "good" faith money, folks.

ANDY: Good-faith money! Not until you raise our trade-in value to $5,500, Bob.

BOB: Folks, I need some up-front cash, before I can "walk" your paperwork to the boss. How about $500?

JOAN: I have five hundred, but here's $20 dollars.

Author's Note: Bob stopped "re-cycling" the Smiths, when he failed to capture any "holding-money" for his in-coming closer. Salesmen measure their selling-prowess, by how much cash [or amount on check] they can seize, from the customer, before releasing them to a closer. In the case of closers, any additional cash [or checks] seized, before the sales manager writes the contract, increases their selling-prowess, too.

At this point, Bob feels he has lost "control" of the Smiths and his near at hand "car-deal" is at a stand still. He leaves the office with lots of paperwork and a twenty dollar bill.

He knows the sales manager will be mad with him. Bob only hopes he didn't mess of things for his incoming closer. The sales manager grabs Bob's messed up deal and calls for a nearby closer. After a short update, they both re-enter Bob's office. Bob seems very distant, though, and limits his action to "blocking" the doorway.

HENRY: High folks, my name is Henry. I'm assisting Bob for the moment. The paperwork looks in order and there's no current problem except for a down-payment check is missing.

JOAN: No problem, we just aren't sure about the deal, especially in respects to our trade-in.

ANDY: [The switch] I think we're making a mistake, honey. Hold on to the check, we're leaving!

HENRY: [Looking angry with Bob] But, folks we are close to making <u>your</u> deal. Don't leave, yet.

ANDY: I think we are over our heads, here, honey. Do you still have that 1994 quality-used car we saw last week? Henry could you check.

BOB:	[Bolting from his post] I don't know, but I thought we had a deal going on the BelchFire.
ANDY:	Who's in charge here?
HENRY:	I'm in charge. Bob, keep quite and go look for the Smiths 1994 quality-used car.
ANDY:	I think we better test drive it, again, honey.
BOB:	No problem. It's here.
JOAN:	I'm hungry. Lets take a break.
ANDY:	Bob, we'll be back in an hour. Just hold on to our paperwork. We'll be back at 7:00 PM. Are you still working the rest of the night?
BOB:	I sure am. I'll have your Q-car, ready!

FADE OUT:

The Director and Writer were too busy with their camera crew to notice the Smiths had already left the dealership for some sandwiches and coffee. Once in the restaurant, though, Andy looked at his watch to notice they had spent two hours with Bob, Henry and the "behind-the-scenes" sales manager, before deciding to "switch" cars to continue with their negotiations, again.

ANDY:	Enough for our practice-run, we "switched" cars to restart the buying process, a new. We told Bob, we would return at 7:00 PM, after a short break. Of course, he didn't believe us. Most salesmen, who let customers "escape," know they will never return to buy a car.
DIRECTOR:	We can actually visualize Bob walking you through his 4-step worksheet. I remember the four-steps are trade-in, price of car, down-payment, and monthly-payments.
JOAN:	When you can visualize their moves, during negotiating, you are in "control," not them.
ANDY:	Of course, we need to work on our plan-of-action, before returning to Bob, Henry and the "hiding" sales manager. Well, did you get an "eye and ear" full of their selling games?

The Writer and Director noticed Bob reacting to Andy's car-lot offer, by "walking" them to his selling-room. Once the Smith's were inside the office, though, the Writer remember the Smith's two-pronged buying plan: "Switching" from the dealer's new BelchFire V9 to the 1994 quality-used car, if Bob was "controllable."

In other words, if Bob can be "controlled," the Smiths would test drive the new car and find several faults with it, during the test-drive. If Bob fielded their questions okay, Andy would continue negotiations with him, by "switching" cars. His "switch" would occur, just after Bob turned-them-over to Henry -- Bob's closer and boss.

Furthermore, once the closer is under "control," the Smiths will continue their negotiations with him, too. Also, Andy planned to consume most of the closer's valuable selling-time with small talk -- chattering. After wasting part of their remain selling-time, Andy will let his cue-cards do their important work: "control" the salesmen's 4-step worksheet, so he may clinch a great bargain in the process.

Looking Ahead:

Andy will eventually flush-out the dealer's "behind-the-scenes" sales manager, and convince him [too] that their deal was the "better" of the two deals! Andy would continue his "battle" with the "aggressive" sale manager and his "sidekicks" the closers, while at the same time catch a quality-used car, for less. Andy knows the closer will try anything and everything to "take" profits from him. Andy doesn't mind that, but "taking" extra money -- deceptively -- from him is not part of his car-buying plan.

6
IN THE SELLING-ROOM, AGAIN

When the Smiths were last seen, they had just concluded their "practice-run" with Bob and Henry at the dealership. The Smiths left both of them to meet the Director and Writer in a nearby restaurant for a quick sandwich and coffee. The Director's last filming sequence showed Bob was running after the Smiths trying to desperately hang onto his "today-buyers," once again. And, Henry was last seen opening the door of the sales office to report to Stan -- the big boss, about Bob's "lose."

Of course, Bob had more at stake then just his time spent on the Smiths. He took valuable selling-time away from other "players" working in Stan's "aggressive" sales-team. Each time Bob re-entered the sales office, he assured everyone the Smith's deal would go through smooth and ease! After the Smiths escaped Bob's "control" of them, The Smiths knew he was in deep trouble with his two bosses! Of course, this was just where Andy wanted Bob to be, as they prepared to go in for the "real deal"-- negotiate for their Q-car, now.

Meanwhile at the restaurant, Andy hands the Director another student handsheet of buying-strategies to review. Since, salesmen have their selling-strategies to "control" the car-buyers with, savvy-buyers should have a few buying-strategies of their own to maintain "control" over their car salesmen. The Director took Andy's buying-strategies and showed them to us:

1. **Plan to spend three-to-four hours negotiating.** If car salesmen are willing to spend three or four hours with potential customers persuading them to sign their contracts. Likewise, car-buyers should be willing to spend extra hours to close their Q-car deals in their favor. Remember, the customer's negotiating starts when the sales manager begins his selling-time "watch." In other words, the first hour with the customer is reserved for putting them on the 4-step worksheet. The remaining two or three hours of selling-time is delegated to the sales manager's quest to "take" any and all customer-cash from them before committing them to a signed contract. For savvy-buyers, the salesman's selling-time is best consumed with small talk or useless chattering. In other words, when the salesmen's selling time is used-up, the sales manager's has less effective selling-time to talk about important parts of the deal -- like the final price of the dealer's car and the dealer's last offer on the buyer's trade-in, if any. Remember too, each time salesmen discuss important figures, take out you cue-cards and slow-down or stop their selling progress when you feel its vital to do so.

2. **Continue to consume selling-time.** When car salesmen and closers leave their offices, they report to sales managers for further instructions for "taking" more profit from their customers. During each of these short-visits -- to the sales office, the "boss" evaluates the minute-to-minute progress achieved, since the last visit. If the car salesmen or closers fail [repeatedly] to yield the desired amount of money the sales manager expects to receive, he will pre-calculate the car-deal's profits in that moment. If the deal has enough profits, the sales manager may close the deal. But, if little or no profits are "apparent" to them,

these "bosses" may give directions to "cycle" the customers, or even send them off the lot. When car salesmen or closers meet savvy-buyers, often they get frustrated at the end of the dealing process -- because of their non-success at "taking" huge profits from them. Even so, sales managers know the importance of selling cars, first, and then counting their profits, later on!

3. Watch for the salesmen's paperwork "magic." It is important to "see" the salesmen's 4-step worksheet, while it's in-motion. Each time the salesman makes his "moves," from one part of the 4-step worksheet to another, he has a reason. Try to "picture" the reason for each of their "moves" in your mind. In other words, each time car salesmen ask for more money, picture where they have moved to on their "worksheet." Savvy-buyers follow the salesman's each "move" by reviewing their cue-cards in the moment. Cue-cards can slow-down or stop most of the car salesman's worksheet "games" or verbal-chattering.

4. "Control" your salesmen with cue-cards. After "switching" to the quality used car desired, cue-cards become the buyer's center-of-reference in the remaining negotiations. Car buying has turned into a contest of talent, between buyer and seller. Many buyers feel it's too much of an ordeal compete and win. Cue-cards change this situation! They are great "equalizers" to the car salesman's continual "verbal" sales-pitches and selling-ploys. Cue cards "act" like poison to most of the car salesmen's game-playing and "tricks." In fact, they spoil their special verbal "bait & switch" strategies often played on buyers. Therefore, car buyers should use their cue-cards to negotiate with. It is suggested "aggressive" car buyers show off their cue-cards, briefly, during the earlier two hours of negotiations. And, when their car-deal's are progressing okay, they should show off their cue-cards, more often!

5. Act unpredictable and uncontrollable. Savvy-buyers prefer car salesmen to follow their buying-plans, not the other way around. In fact, savvy-buyers prefer

acting unpredictable when negotiating with car salesmen. For an example: If a salesman motions you to come with him, just stay where you are, or if the salesman asks for extra money, tell him you have none, or if he asks you lots of questions, answer back with more questions of your own.

6. Bring pencil, paper, calculator, and an extra set of keys. Selling-room cue cards need to be filled-in, while you're negotiating inside the dealer's selling-room. All the negotiating "tools"-- cue cards, pen, paper and calculator must be kept out of the salesmen's reach, at all times. If these items can be reached by the saleman, they may disappear, swiftly. Sometimes, the customer's car keys fail to be returned them. This is because the dealer's appraiser has evaluated their car for possible purchase and has relocated both the car and keys -- out of the owner's reach. Savvy-buyers carry a second set of keys on them, so they can't be held "hostage" very long!

7. Restrict the amount of cash to $500. When car-buyers "flash" their up-front cash, in front of car salesmen, they risk losing it, fast. Car buyers should limit their up-front cash to a few hundred dollars given to car salesmen. This will still allow them to take legal delivery of the dealer's car! Cash binds signed contracts -- between the seller and the buyer, in that very moment. Bear in mind, un-cashed checks are just promissory-notes of future payment. Personal checks lost or not cashed are means, enough, to "break" signed contract's buyer/seller agreements. In other words, the buyer's cash [legal tender], a handshake, and signing of the contract bind all parties -- the buyer and seller to the contract's every word. Another reason for limiting up-front cash given to car salesmen is to restrict their very bad "habit" of moving customer's up-front cash -- elsewhere -- other than for down-payment purposes. All up-front cash released to car salesmen or closers should be restricted to "petty-cash" amounts, until after both parties sign the contract. The reason is obvious! If the car buyer's fails to negotiate a reasonable deal, they will want to leave the dealer.

Andy told both the Director and Writer, these car-buying strategies are both important and worth remembering. With the restaurant-meeting now at its end, they all returned to their positions: The Director and Writer to their listening posts; the Smith's to the movie-set -- new-car dealership.

Playing for Real

The Smiths planned to repeat the same selling-sequence, as they did before with Bob, during their original "practice-run" with him. They will test drive the 1994 quality-used car, again, and then make their car-lot offer to Bob. Then, after making their car-lot offer to Bob, Andy will "walk" him to a nearby office -- the selling-room. Once inside, Andy will re-start his negotiations with Bob and Henry. Joan will stay ready to help Andy, on a moment's notice!

The Writer and Director picked the Smith's action up just after they took the 1994 Q-car for a test drive with their mechanic. It seemed the car checked out, okay. The mechanic found no evidence the Q-car had been mistreated, or that it had been in any accident, previously!

Now, with the Directors ears "glued" to the microphone, Andy and Joan existed their car, to re-start the salesmen's selling-sequences 2 through 10 with Bob who was patiently awaiting for them.

FADE IN

Selling-Step 2: Pre-qualifying & Befriending the Customer

BOB:	Hi folks, the checked out okay, right!
ANDY:	[Bob's following Andy] It has a few problems, but we can talk about them in your office.
JOAN:	The mechanic said the car's transmission had been worked on before. Is that good or bad?
ANDY:	Later, honey.

BOB: The 1994 Q-car is in great demand. They last "forever." This one's going for $15,800 -- includes our <u>special</u> racing-wheel package.

JOAN: Andy, the price seems high? The car at the other dealership was cheaper and had much less miles on it.

BOB: Folks, It's best to avoid used-car dealers. They adjust all the car's mileage records. A popular television program reported 60% of them lie, too, a lot!

ANDY: This seems to be a good running car for both of us, honey.

Selling-Step 3: Walking the Customer to a Office

BOB: Are you sure about this Q-car, folks?

ANDY: I hope so, Bob! The other week, we saw a similar quality-used car selling at $10,500. Why is yours so much higher, Bob?

BOB: I don't know, but you're looking at a fully-loaded car, Andy. The car's in great demand!

JOAN: So is our money in great demand!

ANDY: [Making his car-lot offer] Bob, if you can get me $5,500 for my trade, I'll buy your car for $10,500, now!

BOB: What condition is your car in? Your offer seems very low, but let me see what can be done.

Selling-Step 4: Writing up the Customer

JOAN: [Having a family discussion for Bob's sake] I don't think we should trade it in, just yet.

ANDY: We need the money from the trade to help use with the down payment.

JOAN: But, Andy, I love that car.

BOB: Please, make yourselves comfortable, here. How about some coffee, folks?

ANDY: Yes, I would like my coffee, black, no sugar. Joan prefers...

BOB: [Bob stays put and calls for refreshments] I remember, Joan prefers a coke, right!

JOAN: That's right, thank you. Do you still have our old paperwork, Bob?

BOB: No. I'm afraid Stan had pitched it, last time.

JOAN: Who's Stan?

Selling-Step 5: Starting the 4-Step Worksheet

BOB: Stan! He's our sales managers. Please, I need to see your driver licenses, and credit-data, again, to start your paperwork?

JOAN: Here's a photocopy of it, along with our general application information!

Bob is about to take a sip of coffee, when he notices Andy flipping through a small deck of cards? He ignores what he's seeing, by turning on his fancy calculator machine -- the kind that makes a reassuring clickity-click noises, as if the numbers printed from it come from a much higher source. Bob is smiling, he must be confident of a sale, thought Joan.

As Bob's calculator machine clattered away, Andy took a peek at the Q-car's cue-cards to refresh him memory of the negotiating numbers. Andy smiled as he "witnesses" Bob's writing the $15,800 price figure -- in very-large numbers in the left-top corner of his 4-step worksheet and in the right-top corner he wrote in $3,000 and $1,000 for the trade-in -- but in very-small numbers. He then crossed out the $1,000 figure for the Smiths to see (See Figure 6.1).

TRADE-IN #3,000 ~~$1,000~~	PRICE OF DEALER-CAR - $15,800
DOWN-PAYMENT	MONTHLY-PAYMENTS

FOUR-STEP WORKSHEET
FIGURE 6.1

BOB:	Now, let me put a pen to all this! Our car for $15,800 and your car for $3,000, maybe. Remember, our boss has to okay all these prices first, folks.
ANDY:	$4,000 is low. $5,500 is a better figure, Bob.
BOB:	How much down-payment cash are you going to put down?
JOAN:	$2,000, now.

124

BOB: With $2,000 plus your trade, plus tax and license, your monthly-payments will come to about $504 per month. How's that sound?

JOAN: Why, we would have to stop eating out, honey!

ANDY: Please, slow down a little, Bob. You're talking too fast for us to think about the numbers.

BOB: It's simple, folks. You need to put more cash down on the Q-car to get your monthly payments lower.

ANDY: [Looking worried for Bob's sake] We need lower payments. That's for sure. Why did you write $15,800 when I offered you us a lower price out in the car lot?

BOB: We have to write in the full-retail price of the car for the boss. What if I can get $1,000 off, now, would you buy, today?

ANDY: A thousand dollars off is only a start, Bob. I offered you $10,500 for the car, not $15,800. You need to take better care with your paperwork, Bob.

125

Evidently, Bob ignored Andy's car-lot offer, entirely. He even failed to write down the $1,000 car-lot discount he offered them, too. Joan and Andy remain silent, through, they don't want to push Bob into any corners, yet. First, Andy will expose the cue-cards, just out of Bob's reach, so he can begin to "train" Bob, a little at a time. Next, Andy will refer to his cue-cards, causally, even point to specific spots on them. Finally, these actions will be followed by verbal statements to keep Bob quessing at what will come next. This "training" effort will be subtle reminders Andy is in "control," not Bob (See Figure 6.2).

TRADE: K > $5,500 (WHOLESALE VALUE L > $5,000)	
PRICE OF CAR: I > $10,500 $14,500	$15,800
DOWN: M > $2,000 2/1/.5/.5/	
MONTHLY: N > $10,000 x 36 (10%) = $343	

SELLING-ROOM CUE CARD
FIGURE 6.2

BOB: Lets see, now. $15,800 for our car minus $1,000 off, plus $2,000 down-payment, and.... What if our boss offered you $3,000 for your car, Andy, do we have a deal, then?

ANDY: I thought you mentioned $4,000 before, Bob!

BOB: You did, Andy. If I could get you more, do we have a deal?

ANDY: I need $5,000 for my trade-in, Bob.

BOB: I need more cash, anyway. Can you add another $2,000? Then, maybe I can get more on your trade. Maybe, get your payments down to about $350 plus tax and license. Now that's a great discount!

ANDY: Well, I can give you another $500, but that's it!

BOB: Fine, Let me take your offer to the boss, but I need....

Bob has managed to "push" the Smiths through the 4-Step "worksheet," once. He has taken additional profit -- in the form of extra up-front cash [$500], and he has lowered the Smiths payments -- suggesting a discount has occurred, somewhere in the deal! Now Bob must take his "booty" to the sales manager and "turn-over" the Smiths to a closer.

ANDY: [Andy interrupts] Bob, before you leave, I need to confirm your numbers with mine.

BOB:	Don't worry. But, I do need your down-payment check, now. Do you have it written out, yet?
JOAN:	I have the $500 cash, here, the $2,000 check can wait, Bob.
BOB:	[Reaching for the cash] Well, that will do just nicely.
JOAN:	[Pulling the cash back] Not so fast, buddy! Look but don't touch! If the deal happens, you will get our cash and checks, then.
BOB:	[Shocked] I will give you a receipt. I do need to show the boss, you folks are sincere car buyers.
JOAN:	Here's $20 dollars. How's that?
BOB:	[Takes the twenty-dollar bill] I can make this deal happen for you folks, be back in second.

Entering the Sales-Office Drama:

Bob is in front of Stan -- the sales manager, releasing the Smith's paperwork to him. The boss is asking many "personal" questions about the Smiths to Bob. Bob is loyal to his "boss," answers his questions as a soldier would be if in front of a military general. For Stan is the "top" salesman -- The General In-Charge, and his only mission in life is to "take" profit from individuals who cross his line -- the dealer-ship's property. In other words, when customers show any weakness, or their decision-making seems clouded, he sends in more closers to "bend" these buyers to his way of thinking! And if the customers are strong minded and/or determined to get their way, he sends in specialist closers to "confuse and confound" them -- into believing they got a great deal, then "bend" them to his way of thinking. Sales managers can really put the selling-pressure on both salesmen and customers, alike, with the help of his closer "sidekicks."

STAN:	[Eating ham and cheese sandwich] Well, what you got for me, Bob!
BOB:	Got a live one. Here's their paperwork.

STAN:	Where's their check, mister?
BOB:	They got it. I have $20 dollars, though.
STAN:	[Starring at Bob] How can we "hold" them with $20. Do you got their car keys?
BOB:	Yes.
STAN:	[Appraiser takes keys] It looks weak, Bob. Did you write these high values on the trade? Never mind, step aside! Is Henry working a deal, at the moment? [Over the PA system] Henry, to the sales office.
HENRY:	Yes, sir!
BOB:	Well your boy's got another weak deal going here. I thought you trained your guys, better. Okay [looking in N.A.D.A.], they have a 1991 Q-car, it books out at $4,500 (wholesale), I want you to stay below $3,500. Say anything to get them down. Fortunately, Bob hasn't screwed up our car's selling price, yet. Get me some profit, mister!
HENRY:	Yes, sir. I always win!

Leaving the Sales-Office Drama:

Bob has finished "working" the Smith's deal for now. If Henry gets the Smiths to sign a contract, Bob will get a full-commission for his initial selling-efforts. On the other hand, if Bob had released the Smiths to another salesman, other than his closer-boss, he would be sharing half his commission with another salesman. But, if Henry fails to sign the Smiths to a contract, he will lose his entire portion of the dealer's profit to the closer who signs them. If the second closer fail to get the Smiths to signed, the sales manager will send in other closers, until they sign the Smiths to a contract. Anyway, at this point, the Smiths will be less subtle with Henry, as they negotiate their deal with the behind-the-scenes sales manager. Meanwhile, Henry is studying Bob's awful scribbling on the 4-step worksheet. Here's the deal, as it's structured for the moment (See Figure 6.3).

TRADE-IN	PRICE OF DEALER-CAR
#3,000	$15,800
$1,000	$1,000 OFF
DOWN-PAYMENT	MONTHLY-PAYMENTS
$2,000 CHECK	$504
$500 CASH	$350

FOUR-STEP WORKSHEET

FIGURE 6.3

<u>Selling-Step 6: Turning-Over the Customer</u>

HENRY:	Mr. & Mrs. Smith, my name is Henry Sterling. Bob will be back later on. I've looked your paperwork over. Did you know your credit union complained about receiving late-payments from you, last year!
JOAN:	I don't think that would impact our credit rating, very much?
HENRY:	Let me see what I can do. If I can get your interest rate to 18%. Do we have a deal?
ANDY:	[Looking at cue-card] Lower rates would be better, Henry.
HENRY:	Our bank will extend your loan to 48 months, at these rates.
JOAN:	Don't you think 48 months is too long, Andy?
ANDY:	[Henry hears] Lower payments are important.
BOB:	[Enters office] Here's the Smith's trade-in appraisal sheet, Mr. Sterling.

131

HENRY:	[To shock] Your trade came in at $3,200. Now that's great news, Andy. Plus your $2,500 cash down will lower your payments, further.
ANDY:	[Looking at cue-cards] I can write another check for $1,000. But, I need more money for my trade-in.
HENRY:	1991 Q-cars just aren't selling well! At last week's auction a 1991 Q-car, loaded, sold for $3,100.
JOAN:	Our car is loaded. I saw one on the street going for five thousand, just last week.
HENRY:	[Interrupting Joan] What if I could get you $3,200 for the trade. Do we have a deal?
ANDY:	No. We need more.
HENRY:	Let me take your down-payment check and cash to the boss, and see what he decides.
JOAN:	I'll keep the check and cash in my purse, thank you. You have our $20 dollars?
HENRY:	[Getting up to leave] Okay, let me see what I can do for you folks.

Entering the Sales Office Drama:

STAN: You got me more money, right?

HENRY: Of course, $1,000 more cash down.

STAN: Where's it at, mister?

HENRY: They have it, but I got them talking monthly payments, again, and I'll get more off them, soon.

STAN: We've put several hours into them. Get more cash-down and commit them to buy, today.

Leaving the Sales Office Drama:

Henry leaves the sales office still confident of a sale with the Smiths. On the hand, the Smiths, are confident of "controlling" Bob and Henry, and believe they will "bend" these salesmen to their way of thinking, eventually.

HENRY: Let me see, now. Our car for $14,800 and yours for $3,200. This includes our special rims and wheels package, too.

ANDY: [Looking at cue-cards] We offered $10,500 for your car, and want $5,000, for ours!

HENRY: What if I can get your payments to $320, now that sounds like another chunk off our car!

ANDY: Sounds great, but my concern is with my car, at the moment. I need more for it.

HENRY: Okay! Give me more down-payment cash, and I will present your offer to the boss, again!

ANDY: [Looking at cue-cards] We only have $500 cash on me. We need more for my trade-in.

JOAN: I'll keep our $500 cash and two checks tucked safely away, here. If a deal is made, and our contract gets signed, I'll release them to you.

HENRY: I need to bring more than just paperwork to my boss. Maybe, some more petty cash.

ANDY: Look, try and make the deal happen, Henry, we're getting very tired of negotiating, here.

Andy flips to his selling-room cue-card and updates it for us all to see, as Henry rushes out of the office to report to Stan (See Figure 6.4).

TRADE: K > $5,500

  (WHOLESALE VALUE L > $5,000   )

PRICE OF CAR: I > $10,500 $15,800

$14,500

DOWN: M > $2,000ck+$500 cash + $1,000 ck

  2/1/.5/.5/

MONTHLY: N >$10,000 x 36 (10%) = $343

SELLING-ROOM CUE CARD

FIGURE 6.4

Entering the Sales-Office Drama:

STAN: Henry, what have you got, mister!

HENRY: I got two today-buyers, ready to sign!.

STAN: How much cash did you get from them?

HENRY: None, sir!

STAN: Where's the checks and cash at? We can't "hold" people with petty cash, mister!

HENRY: I got their trade-in low -- below wholesale, and interest rates high. They are very easy to "control," at this point.

STAN: I'm not sure who's in control here. Henry, your job is to "take" profit. Where is it? Now, keep them at $3,200 for their trade-in, and don't go below $14,000 for our car. Don't lose them!

Leaving the Sales-Office Drama:

Henry is getting worried. He seems to be getting nowhere with the Smiths. His boss wants to get the show on the road, and the Smiths don't seem to be in a hurry to buy their car. Henry enters the room, and then turns on the calculator to continue negotiations with the Smiths.

HENRY: Well, the boss helped us out, folks. I got our 1994 quality-used car down to $14,800. Now, isn't that good news!

ANDY: Not really, Henry.

HENRY: For the bad news, the boss can't offer more than $3,200 for your car. Also, he wants the two checks for $3,000 and the $500 cash, too.

JOAN: I think we need to go, elsewhere, honey. Obviously, Stan doesn't want to "trade" cars with us, today.

HENRY: Folks, I'm on your side, really! If I can get your payments to $300, are you interested?

ANDY: [Looking at cue-cars] I don't want to talk about lower monthly payments. I'm stuck with getting more for my trade! [Andy is showing Joan the cue-cards] I believe, my figures are correct. *The N.A.D.A. Official Used Car Guide* stated my trade was worth $5,000 wholesale and your car worth around $11,000, maximum! Can you tell me who is at error, here?

HENRY: That's easy. The "N.A.D.A." doesn't set any dealer's prices, it only gives average prices of auctioned cars, around the country. Their numbers are way out-of-date. Now, look at these auction sheets, for just a minute. They give you the "real" picture of what car are worth. See how low 1991 Q-cars are!

ANDY: [Staring at the sheets] Okay! I think we had better go, Joan. Thanks for your help Henry and yours too, Bob [Bob's blocking doorway].

HENRY: Wait. I have a great idea. I'll run this one by boss, maybe he help us out, a little.

Entering the Sales-Office Drama:

STAN: Well that didn't take long! How much....

HENRY: [Interrupting Stan] These guys are tough! They have some kind of paperwork of their own. I can't get them to talk payments nor get any money off them.

STAN: You're weak! The Smiths look very normal, to me! I got $10,500 in the car plus $1,800 in rims and wheels. I need $13,800 for the car!

HENRY: They are locked in at $10,500, Sir! I can't seem to budge them.

STAN: They're bluffing. Get my figures put on their contract or I'll send in Hank -- The hatchet!

HENRY: I can do it. Let me try one more time.

STAN: Okay, but don't lose them or my $1,800 rims and wheels package, either!

Leaving the Sales-Office Drama:

Henry has one more chance to "work" the Smiths. If he fails, Stan will be sending another closer to deal with them. For a look at Henry's 4-step worksheet (See Figure 6.5).

TRADE-IN	PRICE OF DEALER-CAR
#3,000 ~~$1,000~~ + $200 appraisal $3,200 max	$15,800 $1,000 OFF $14,800
DOWN-PAYMENT	MONTHLY-PAYMENTS
$2,000 CHECK $500 CASH $1,000 CHECK	~~$500~~ ~~$350~~ $300 18%

FOUR-STEP WORKSHEET
FIGURE 6.5

HENRY: The boss didn't help much, Andy. He checked the costs in the 1994 Q-car, and he's stuck with $14,000!

ANDY: What about my car?

HENRY: I could only get $300 more for it! But, your payments are much lower, because our bank has cleared your loan papers for 60 months!

ANDY: Forget payments, for the moment. It's better to take out my trade to simplify your deal. Now, talk about your 1994 quality-used car's selling price! Appearently, it's high because of a special rims and wheels package on it. What did you say its worth was?

HENRY: The boss adds new rims and wheels on every used-car he sells because of their insurance.

137

	It adds real value to the quality-used cars for about $1,800.
ANDY:	I don't need your special rims and wheels package. I want the car's original tires put back on, and $1,800 taken off your car's $14,800 asking price.
HENRY:	[Looking stressed out] I don't know if the old tires can be put back on. I'll be right back. If you need anything Bob will help you.

Entering the sales-office drama:

STAN:	You lost my rims and wheels package!
HENRY:	I didn't mean to. It was the Smiths idea. They know something.
STAN:	I'm sending in the Hatchet man! Give me the Smith's paperwork, and go look for some used rims and wheels, quickly!
HANK:	Yes, sir!

STAN: We have four hours, in these folks, and Henry can't seem to budge them -- to our way of thinking. See what you can do for us.

Hank reviews the Smith's credit application and the 4-step worksheet for any discrepancies. It looks all okay to him! Bob had cycled them properly, Henry had recycled them, twice. What was the Smith's problem, anyway. Let's take a look at the current status of the 4-step worksheet, before Hank re-enter and "work" the Smiths (See Figure 6.6).

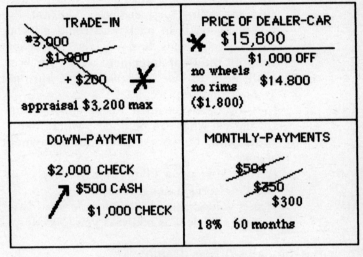

FOUR-STEP WORKSHEET

FIGURE 6.6

Leaving the sales-office drama:

HANK: Hi folks! My name is Hank Troy. Now, lets see. If I understand everything, correctly, Henry is looking for the Q-car's rims and wheels. After examining your paperwork, I can't find what you agreed to. Did Henry tell you the problems with your trade? What if I could get you $4,000, would you buy, today?

139

JOAN:	My husband has taken the trade out of the deal, Hank. It's too late to negotiate for it!
HANK:	I see. Well, If the boss lowers his car to $13,500, do we have a deal, then?
JOAN:	We have $3,500 down payment! We are today-buyers, Hank. All you need to do is agree to our $10,500 offer for your 1994 Q-car.
HANK:	The boss can't go that low.
JOAN:	You have our twenty dollars, where is our receipt for it?
ANDY:	[Looking at cue-cards] I have been careful with my figures, Hank. 1994 quality-used cars are selling for just under $11,000. I've taken my trade-in back, and removed your car's special rims and wheels package to simplify the final agreement with your boss. I still want to buy the 1994 Q-car, but only at a reasonable price.
HANK:	[Getting up to leave] It's near closing time. Let me see what can be done. I would like to show Stan, our boss, your down-payment check!
JOAN:	[Writes void on a blank check] Here! Your checking service can confirm if it's good.
HANK:	[Takes voided-check] Okay, let me try. I want to close this deal as badly as you folks do.

Entering the sales-office drama:

STAN:	Why are they stuck on these same numbers?
HANK:	I can't bump them off their numbers. They have some information-cards or something, in their hands.
STAN:	Can't you loose them?
HANK:	No! Either Andy or Joan has them, always.
STAN:	I have too much time invested in them, now!
HANK:	Sir. They have paper, pencil, and calculator, too! I think they are really cash-buyers not payment-buyers, as Henry and Bob believed.

STAN:	It took a long time to discover that, mister! I pay you guys to stay in "control" of my customers, and not the other way around.
HANK:	They are stuck on $10,500 for our 1994 car!
STAN:	Okay. I need $12,000. Don't lose them!

Leaving the sales-office drama:

This may be the last time Hank has to "work" the Smiths. Stan looked very upset with his non-performance, so far. Maybe he'll get lucky and "sign" the Smiths on a contract, this time around.

HANK:	[Meeting the Smiths in the hall] The boss lowered his price to $12,000. He needs $500 profit on the 1994 Q-car to show the owners, tomorrow. Now, that sounds great to me. What do you folks got to say?
ANDY:	We'll keep the rims and wheels, and I'll split the difference to $11,000.

HANK:	This car books for $15,000 with the rims and wheels on it! Don't lose this great deal for such a little difference of opinion.
ANDY:	It's 10:00 PM, I hope your boss can agree to our <u>last</u> offer. Honey, lets get ready to leave.
JOAN:	Hand me your cue-cards, pen and calculator.
HANK:	Okay you got a deal -- $11,000 and our rims and wheels, today. I need your down-payment checks and cash for our boss, so he can confirm all the numbers and make ready the final contract for signing.
JOAN:	I will release them, after a contract is signed by all parties, thank you.
HANK:	[Leaving the office] Bob, call me if they try and leave, again. Don't you know what your job is by now!

Entering the sales-office drama:

Now, Hank is sweating across his upper lip, just like Nixon did when he lost his government job as the president of the United States.

STAN:	What have you got for me?
HANK:	A "thin" deal, sir.
STAN:	Where's my $12,000 car deal, down-payment checks and cash at? Hank, I'm disappointed.
HANK:	These people are really sensitive characters. I almost lost them a few minutes a go.
STAN:	Listen, you take the Smiths to another closing-room and close my deal, you know the one I like, or else!

Leaving the sales-office drama:

Moving the Smiths to another selling-room and having the same closer re-work them is not typical. Stan should of "fired" Hank in front of the other salesmen working for him, then go in and "work" the Smiths himself!

HENRY: Well folks, your deal seems to be approved. I need to take you over to our computer-room, so the contract figures can be re-confirmed and placed on a contract for all to sign.

ANDY: It sounds like we have another car, honey.

FADE OUT:

A Tentative-Deal made:

The Director, Writer and camera crew were all jubilant about the Smith's apparent "victory" over Stan and his selling-team. It looked so easy, because the Smiths reviewed their cue-cards throughout negotiations. The Director and Writer now understand how Andy's cue-cards reduced the car salesmen's ability to complicate negotiations, in front of them. Even Stan -- the sales manager, could not confuse or confound the Smiths from the sales office. What surprised everyone in the camera-crew, was Stan's judgment to "take" his profits and without any concern for his selling-team or the buyers, themselves. Maybe, the public's bad opinion of car salesmen was incorrect, and that the blame should be placed on the backs of "aggressive" sales managers and closers not front-line car salesmen, thought the Director.

LOOKING AHEAD:

The Writer tried to restructure the Smith's next moves: The Smiths would continue "controlling" Bob, Henry, Stan with their cue-cards; they would study the upcoming contract, from top to bottom, and make all necessary changes not consistent with their cue-card data; and finally they would re-examine the 1994 Q-car, before leaving the car lot, just in case the dealer's mechanics tried to remove or change anything on it, during their negotiations.

7
IN THE CLOSING ROOM

As the curtain came down on the last act, Bob, Henry and even Hank had announced they <u>all</u> were ready to close the Smith's deal for real. The sales-team announced the good news as if it was reality. But really, each salesman had "washed" their hands of the Smith's deal, only the final closer needed to write-up their contract for their review and signatures. The Smiths knew many an unwary buyer who had dropped their guard -- at that point, would suffer serious financial consequences, later on. The Smiths had no intention of letting their guard down. Not for one minute! They would not relax, until after they had signed and took delivery of the 1994 quality-used car. Their experiences at buying cars from car dealers have taught the Smiths the stakes keep going up when inside the dealer's closing-room!

Up to now, all the terms Bob, Henry and Hank have quoted the Smiths have been put on a 4-step worksheet, and not on a real contract of any kind. In fact, sales managers consider the 4-step worksheet more like a "soft" contract -- anything can be changed. In other words, nothing is "termed" final, until after the sales manager signs for it.

Special Closers Write Up Sales Contracts:

Most dealers use specialist-closers to write their contracts. And, the finance/insurance room is the sales manager's last "chance" to gain additional profits, before the contract gets written and then signed by both parties. Therefore, special closers are assigned the task of converting their salesmen's "worksheets" into finished contracts for all to "witness" and sign them. Only "top" closers get the chance to commit customers to signed-contracts. Sales managers call them F/I managers. If the sales manager instructs them to "recycle" the customer -- for additional profit-taking, they remain loyal to their "boss's" instructions right to the letter. This is exactly what Andy and Joan expect from Stan the man!

Andy and Joan know they must be very alert despite the last closer's jovial "It's just about wrapped up folks" demeanor. The Smiths understand the terms on the "soft" contract are not final, until after it has been converted into a "hard" contract by the F/I manager and made ready for signing. After all, when one signs any contract, the law of the land locks in, every sentence, paragraph and page of it.

Many car buyers have negotiated excellent deals with their salesmen just like Andy and Joan. Then, several weeks later, they decide to re-read their active [signed] contracts, only to discover [too late] different terms have been put on it. Andy has heard of cases, where sales managers request customers to sign first. Then they make several changes on the [signed] contract, before returning it to their customers. Always, Andy asks the sales manager to sign, first, before continuing to review, initial and sign the contract. And to be assured of no future difficulties, Andy takes his carbon-copy off the contract in that very moment.

Author's Note: Some car dealers have "specialist-closers" to handle their after-sale customers, too. These closers have the task of resolving all disputes, but in the favor of the dealer. For example: If a car dealership's accounting manager failed to "push" a recently "sold" customer-contract to an outside financing company, the "specialist-closer" must contact the "sold" customer and demand the return of both the "sold" car and carbon-copy of the contract. These closers then, in the interest of their dealer, legally "un-wind" the customer's deal and take back the "sold" car. Another example: After the sale, a customer's loan gets declined, because of insufficient down-payment cash attached to their financing paperwork. The closer will probably demand additional up-front cash from the "sold" customer, and/or "switch" them into another car -- cheaper, but this time with an more expensive contract attached to it.

Rules for Closing a Deal in Your Favor:

The Smiths have seven more buying-strategies for safely steering through the finance/insurance-room maze, and onto the final signing of a contract. They are the last "rules" a car buyer will need to remember to beat the salesman at his own "con" game.

1. Restate agreed-upon figures, often. Take the cue-cards out, and tell the F/I manager what was previously agreed-upon: on the car price, down-payment, the trade-in amount [if any] and monthly-payments [if any]. Car buyers must re-confirm every quoted-number a salesman or closer, or F/I manager presents to them, before they continue negotiations with the sales manager. If quotes are different, in any way, the car buyer must make the salesman or closer or F/I manager correct them, right on the spot!

In many cases, the F/I manager may ignore the customer, during the initial moments of conversation. Don't get upset, just repeat the previously agreed-upon figures, until the sales manager [hiding inside the sales office] "signals" the F/I manager to <u>stop</u> "recycling" the customer and finally agree to the agreed-upon terms they keeps on repeating.

After a few "foiled" attempts to confuse or confound the car buyer, most F/I managers will finally write their customer's contracts -- in finished form, unchanged, and ready for reviewing and signing.

Cue-cards provide you only means of repeating your agreed-upon terms during the negotiating process. Cue-cards help maintain "control" over the sales manager and F/I manager. Cue-cards put the power where it belongs -- in the hands of consumers. Finally, it's difficult for "specialist" closers to confuse or confound savvy-buyers, after the sale, when they have their cue-cards with them.

2. Make sure all figures are correct. Use the cue-cards to "review" the final figures on the contract. For example: The car's price reads $12,500 on the contract. But the buyer agreed to $11,000. The buyer should ask the F/I manager -- why the difference, and then demand it changed back to what is on the buyer's cue-cards. No matter what these salesmen say or do, get the figures changed to the agreed-upon amounts or leave the dealership! The same goes for the down-payment and/or any deposited cash [if any] you gave them, and/or the trade-in's price, if a trade-in is involved. The reason is obvious. The four pricing areas: trade-in price, price of car, down-payment and cash deposit, are the vital parts of a signed contract.

If the contract gets too confusing as the F/I manager reviews it in front of the buyer, they should ask him to slow down. Also, when the buyer is reviewing the final contract, they should pull their cue-cards, paper and pencil before them. Then when one of the four-price figure are mentioned, have the F/I manager point to its location on the contract. Remember, the four-pricing figures are: Trade-in value, Price of car, Down-payment amount, and Monthly-payments figure. After reviewing the four "vital" figures, write down any other numbers the F/I manager quotes from the contract onto a separate piece of paper. Now with this piece of paper in-front of the buyer, ask the F/I manager to slowly discuss each of these "other" terms/figures, until the buyer is totally convinced each term/figure belongs on the contract.

3. **Make sure all the selling-room promises are written on the contract.** Remember, most salesmen's promises are just verbal "bait & switch" chattering, and often nothing more. If the salesman's verbal-promises aren't placed on paper, the salesmen will conveniently forget them, later on. Savvy-buyers write down all their salesmen's verbal-promises on the back of their cue-cards or on the back of their business cards. Once any car salesmen "see" their verbal chatter going on paper, they usually get tongue-tied, fast. Also, if car buyers take their time to write them down, those verbal-promises made by car salesmen can be of future use. In other words, by re-reading verbally-made-promises by previously met salesmen, the F/I manager may try to re-adjust the buyer's contract, but in their favor. Usually, the F/I manager will call in the car salesmen "responsible," and attempt to resolve the matter, to every-one's satisfaction. Not only will this consume more selling "time" in the closing-room, it may result in a few verbal promises coming true for car buyers -- who dare to ask!

4. **Remove non-essential charges off the contract.** Non-essential charges don't mean tax and license fees. Non-essential charges mean: dealer documentation fees, service warrantees with extra-high premiums attached to them, detail-servicing contracts of little consumer value added on, and/or auto-insurance premium issued from "mail-order" type insurance companies. For example: If the sales manager believe their customer still has extra cash on them, they may "instinctively" attempt to re-distribute it somewhere else -- in places that benefit the dealer the most. In other words, when a customer's extra cash gets dispersed into add-ons like service contracts and/or insurance policy premiums, the customer's original cash down-payment is reduced, accordingly. Meanwhile the car-deal's profit-margin skyrockets. Sales managers that actually re-locate a buyer's money to "non-essential" areas of the car-deal

and/or contract, usually are awarded bigger percentages of the car dealer's total sales-profits.

5. Stop "distracting" tactics used by F/I Manager. Salesmen often use distracting-tactics with their customers, during the contract-reviewing session. When F/I managers use such distracting-tactics as speeding-up or covering-up portions of the contract during the reviewing of the contract, they are probably hiding something from their customers. Or, when F/I managers bring several salesmen into the closing-room during the reviewing of the contract, they probably have something to hide from the customer, too. No matter what distracting-tactics are used, if any, the buyer must stop the F/I manager at each paragraph during the contract-reading session, no exceptions. In other words, after each paragraph is read and understood, the buyer should then direct the F/I manager to continue with the contract-reading session.

6. When salesmen use intimidation to sell cars. If F/I managers change their attitude with their customers by referring to them as "being stupid" for not understanding the contract, they are probably hiding something from the customer. Or, when F/I managers or specialist-closers sell cars via "intimidation," buyers should just be wary and leave the car dealership. It is common for "aggressive" car salesmen to "bully" customers inside their [private] selling and closing rooms. Especially, after car salesmen and closers discover how to financially "manipulate" their clientele inside the dealer's selling and closing-rooms. This happens to salesmen who get "greedy" or see the ease of taking "huge" profits from other -- just for the fun of it! To make matters even worse, sales managers praise these "creative" salesmen with daily/weekly cash-awards for doing such a good job at selling. Finally, the greatest cash-award for "top" closers [never a front-line car salesman] is to someday be selected the dealer's latest sales manager! When savvy-buyers encounter these "creative" car seller's, they usually leave for the next dealer-car location!

7. Never take delivery of car, until the contract is certain. It may seem a foolish statement, but many people have received their cars and contracts only to have returned them both [car and contract] to the dealer's a few days later because of financing problems or contract errors.

With these seven car-buying strategies kept in mind, the Writer and Director returned to their listening/viewing posts to "witness" the final "act" of Joan and Andy's car-buying plan.

F/I-Room Action Begins:

Arriving in the F/I-room, Hank reached in the desk's top-drawer for some pre-printed contract-forms. He hopes the Smiths have forgotten the tentative-car deal made, earlier. Hank plans to "re-cycle" the Smiths -- on paper, again, then he will write their final contract when Stan gives the okay to do so. Andy's buying-strategy is to open his negotiations with a bang! He will expose the cue-cards more openly. He reviews the 1994 Q-car's selling-room cue card, now. Here is what it looks like (See Figure 7.1).

TRADE: K > $~~5,500~~   no trade (WHOLESALE VALUE L > $5,000   )
PRICE OF CAR: I > $~~10,500~~ $11,000+ wheels $~~15,800~~   & rims $14,500
DOWN: M > $~~2,800~~ck+$~~500~~cash + $1,000 ck 2/1/.5/.5/ $3,500 d/p max.
MONTHLY: N >$10,000 x 36 (10%) = $343

SELLING-ROOM CUE CARD

FIGURE 7.1

153

FADE IN

HANK:	Okay! $3,000 in checks and $500 cash-down payment, and our 1994 Q-car for $12,500. Sounds like a great deal to me, Andy.
ANDY:	[Looking at cue-cards] Actually, it's our check and cash for $3,500, and your Q-car for $11,500, Hank.
HANK:	Ah, yes, Andy. My paperwork is in such a mess, at the moment. What if I can get $4,000 for your Trade?
JOAN:	The Trade is not for sale.

Even though Andy and Joan can detect Hank's weak attempt to "recycle them through the numbers, again, they continue with their positive attitude of Hank to keep the dealing process going foreword. Right now, Hank's scratching ink-pen, has Andy on his seat's edge. He is getting tired of competing with such an "aggressive" group of "salesmen." Joan spots Andy's attitude, changed, and offers to help him by reviewing Hank's numbers, more closely.

JOAN:	What's this $486 for?
HANK:	Our extended warrantee on your 1994 Q-car.
JOAN:	We don't need an extended warrantee. How long is your used-car warrantees, anyway?
HANK:	We guarantee our cars for 90-days.
JOAN:	Where is this discussed in the contract?
HANK:	Our warrantees are discussed on the back of the final contract.
JOAN:	Like I said, we don't need to pay for any additional warrantees.
ANDY:	Maybe so ,if the car was six or seven year-old, but for a three year old. No thank you.
HANK:	Are you folks going to need financing?
ANDY:	Depends on your rates, Hank.

Hank searches through his paperwork to find the 4-step worksheet. He's somewhat relieved about the Smith's new interest in car loans. Hank likes to talk monthly payments with them, because he may get another chance to "take" extra dealer-profits to Stan the man!

HANK:	Let me see... The 1994 Q-car is three years old. I think our loan company will go 16%. How's that sound, folks?
JOAN:	Well, if that's the best you can do. Did you replace the rims and wheels, yet?
HANK:	I don't know.
ANDY:	Well, you need to find the wheels. We can't buy it without wheels.
HANK	For the moment, I need to clear all these numbers with the boss. I'll be right back.

Entering the Sales-Office Drama:

STAN:	Well, mister!
HANK:	I got high interest rates on $7,500.
STAN:	It's too late to talk interest rates. Try our service contracts and warrantees on them.
HANK:	I tried that, earlier. Every time I talk about price or trade or any add-on, they refer to some little cheat sheets. I can't add or take away from the deal with these "cards" in their possession. They asked about our car's rims and wheels?
STAN:	It's too late to change tires, mister. I'm going in to add some profit in this deal. Step aside, mister!

Leaving the Sales-Office Drama:

Stan plans to offer the Smiths a small gift, an auto-detailing package, in exchange for a much higher price on the 1994 Q-car. He hopes to close the Smith's deal in a few minutes.

STAN:	How are you folks?
ANDY:	We're fine, thank you. Do you have the final contract written up, yet?

STAN: There's one small problem. We have too much in the car to let it go for $11,000. I just can't release it. The car's rims and wheels are too valuable! The good news is car-financing arrangements have been set at 16%. I need $12,000 for my car to make it all happen.

ANDY: [Looking at cue-cards] Like I told, Bob, Henry, Hank and now you, we don't have more cash. The down-payment is coming from my father, and now I have to keep my trade-in and try and resell it, just to pay my father back.

STAN: My car for $12,000, you keep the rims and wheels on the car, and I'll include our auto-detailing package [$500 value added package] for free.

ANDY: Well, thanks for trying. It's now 10:30 PM! It's really late for us. We need to go home and feed the dog. Honey, are you ready?

JOAN:	Oh, be sure to thank Bob and Henry and Hank, for us! Goodbye Stan.
STAN:	[Interrupting Andy] I have only one idea left. How about $12,000 even?
ANDY:	I wish I could, but I can't put another dime on my credit cards, right now! I'm stuck with my earlier offer of $10,000, and you keep your rims and wheels, thank you.
STAN:	But, I have $1,800 in them!
ANDY:	I think way less, Stan. You get them for below wholesale and sometimes for free, right!
STAN:	[A very long pause] Well, not exactly. The wheels are quality stuff, you know!
ANDY:	I guess we better go. Do you have our $20?
STAN:	I think we are close, folks. Okay! The 1994 Q-car for $11,000 with rims and wheels, as is, for your $3,500 down-payment plus 16% car loan -- the balance on a three year loan.
ANDY:	Sounds good to me. What do you think, Joan?
JOAN:	If everything reads okay on the contract, yes.

Entering the Sales-Office Drama:

HANK:	[Looking at Stan] I didn't say anything, sir.
STAN:	You're right, they have some kind of "cards" in their hands. I tried to get my rims and wheels back, and lost them and free detailing-service contract, too. What is our world coming to?
HANK:	Are you going to let them "walk?"
STAN:	No! Close their deal, now, before something else goes wrong.
HANK:	[This happens rarely, these days!] It's those "how to" car-buying books that hurt us, so!
STAN:	I'll be the laughing stock, tomorrow. I bet Andy sold cars in the past. Usually, I can smell them a mile away. How many man-hours have we put into these two, anyway?
HANK:	Well, if you add up Bob's, Henry's, mine and your time spent -- together, we have eight-man hours on them.
STAN:	I have a bad feeling about that high-interest rate with the loan company. You left Bob with the Smiths, right?

Leaving the Sales-Office Drama:

HANK:	Well folks, finally your contract has arrived. Now, lets read the contract through. Please mark your initials on the right-side of the contract -- next to each paragraph. Ready!
ANDY:	[Looking at cue-cards while Hank reviews] Hank, where is the car's price of $11,000 and $3,500 down-payment figures at?
HANK:	Right here and there. Also, our manager gave you a one-year detailing service for free! He's a nice guy, you know!
JOAN:	Where is that written in your the contract?
HANK:	Our dealer-service contracts are on separate paper, Mrs. Smith.

JOAN:	Not good enough. We need it written on the contract -- itself, including our four rims and wheels package, too.
HANK:	[Wasting no time, he writes it in] Okay, I have noted per your request, the detailing-service and the rims & wheels package at the bottom of the contract. Now, the balance due is $7,500 for 36 months at 18%. Initial here, here, and here, here, here and here please.
ANDY:	Your payments come to $260.25. Initial here, here, and here. That's right, before the boss changes his mind. Okay, how will you pay for your tax and license fees, folks?
JOAN:	I'll right another check for it. Here's our down-payment checks and $500 cash deposit.
ANDY:	Oh, before you leave, Hank, call your boss in, so he can sign on the contract, too.
JOAN:	Also, we need a copy of the contract, and our $20 dollars returned to us.
HANK:	What $20 dollars?????

JOAN:	The $20 dollar bill we gave Bob, earlier.
HANK:	[On the telephone asking for Stan] Folks, he will be right in.
JOAN:	[Both Andy and Joan get up] We'll meet you out on the car lot, then. Where are our cars?
ANDY:	[Checking both cars] Well everything looks good.
JOAN:	[Opens trunk] We need a spare tire, Andy.
STAN:	[Walking the Smiths back to the office] Folks, I'll get you a spare put in, right now. Now it's getting late. Here's your twenty dollars back.
ANDY:	[Everyone is standing, now] Well done, Joan. I guess we have another car to take care of.
JOAN:	No, you have another car to take care of.
ANDY:	Well, thank you for doing business with us, Stan. It was quit an experience for us.
STAN:	Likewise, and thank you for coming in, today.

FADEOUT

Summing Up:

After Joan and Andy signed their contract, everybody left the dealer's closing-room. Even Bob left his post -- the room's doorway and "walked" with the Smiths to their cars. Both cars were waiting at the dealer's main exit. Andy noticed they had pasted on the car's DMV registration I.D. on the front-windshield. The Writer and Director were jumping up and down, across the street, excited about the Smith's victory over Stan the man! Only the Smiths noticed all the commotion with the movie crew across the street. Apparently, Bob, Henry, Hank and Stan were just too busy, chaining up the dealer's entrance and exits for the night, to have noticed the Smith's celebration by the "audience."

The next day, Andy plans to finish his business with Stan the man! Evidently, Andy has made previous car-loan arrangements with his credit union because he is a member and their rates are the lowest. Andy's credit union line of credit seemed a logical step because the older 1991 Q-car may take extra time to resell at his price. Then when it does resell, Andy will pay-down his credit-union loan.

In the afternoon on the same day, Andy went to the credit union to talk with their loan officer about the dealer's contract-amount. After a short discussion with their loan arranger, a cashier's check was drafted for $7,500 in the dealer's name. Andy received the cashier's check and signed their loan papers at 8 percent for one year.

On the very same day -- in the late-afternoon, Andy with check and copy of contract in his hand returned to the new-car dealership. Andy located the dealer's accounting-office manager and told him that he wanted to pay-off a recently signed contract on a 1994 quality-used car, now! Of course, the account manager processed Smith's paperwork, swiftly, and after quick confirmation of the cashiers-check, he then stamped all the copies of the contract "paid-in-full." Andy's copy was returned him and the account-manager thanked him for doing business with them. By paying the dealer's contract off, now, Andy had saved another twelve percent on a $7,500 loan by "switching" loan companies.

After returning home, Andy felt very satisfied with his "victory" of Stan the man. In two years, Andy would get to meet more "aggressive" car salesmen when it came trade-in time, again. And of course, he couldn't take all the credit for the "victory," Joan and his father's cue-card system really did most of the work.

Epilogue:

Andy prepared his 1991 Q-car for re-sell, by having it detailed in a local shop for $50 dollars. He then placed classified-ad on the car for $5,800. After seven customer "offers," the car sold at $5,300. Andy, then closed the 1991 Q-car's file, after realizing it cost him $1200 plus gas, oil, and maintenance in the three years he owned and drove it. Andy believes $400 per year to own a recently new car is a fair price to pay! Next time, though, he will resell the 1994 Q-car, much sooner!

Meanwhile, Joan has been enjoying her three-year old Q-car. She is always proud of her husband's car buying skills. In fact, she faxed Andy's father a letter to tell him of Andy's performance with Stan, Hank, Henry, and Bob. She especially liked Bob's manners, though, maybe because of his "innocent" looking face. She will send him a Christmas card this year, for usre!

One year later:

Shortly after the Director released his movie to the public, Bob got promoted to a closer's position by the dealer's new-owners. He was promoted because of his "honest" approach with his customers. Meanwhile, Henry replaced the now missing Stan the man, because he was doing "good-behavior" at some local camp for his "involvement" in the now "famed" car-buying documentary. The Director's movie "exposed" many of the car salesmen's selling-tactics, especially, the old fashined "baiting & switching" games still being played by veteran car salesmen. Eventually, thought, the Director's movie proved most useful in court against "aggressive" car salesmen who continued practicing their ancient "selling-arts" of the 50,s and 60's -- confusing and confounding the general public for profit-taking reasons. Finally, the Director became a famous consumer-crusader, in his own time. In fact, it was last reported, the Director and Writer were both searching the high Andes, in Chile, for Andy's father for a second movie script on new-car leasing scams!

8
The Workshop

Andy's Cue-Card System:

So now you know how Joan and Andy beat the car salesman at his own game. You probably figure you can do it, too! Before you start mixing it up with the pros, though, here is Andy's seven-step workshop to help make sure you're ready to compete with "aggressive" car salesmen in the market. Andy has tried to make each task, in the workshop, both helpful and effective to the car buyer. Sort of a one-stop shopping guide. Andy urges everyone to search for only quality-used cars with high-resell values at the library. Andy's experience with students, though, have indicated most individuals have prematurely made up their minds to which cars interest them. Even so, Andy still suggests buyers not bypass the two library tasks required to successfully complete his workshop. It is very important car buyers pre-document their car-of-choice's "true" resell-values before attempting to buying them! Remember, buying the wrong car at any price is a poor "investment."

Also, Andy recommends buyers divide their car-buying tasks into two separate phases: a "practice" phase -- in which the buyer practices their negotiating skills on a few car salesmen from their shopping-list, and second, a "car-buying" phase -- in which the buyer negotiates for one of their "top" car choices on the shopping-list. If the buyers are impatient persons, they might be tempted to rush in, unprepared. Be forewarned, here! Thousands of hard earned consumer-dollars are at stake -- when buyers face car salesmen, unprepared! Car salesmen practice their verbal "traps" on every customer they encounter. Car salesmen are always ready, everyday, to compete with consumers! And, if the buyer's time is so important, just think about the few hours spent "practicing" a few car salesmen -- the buyer's opponents, could save them thousands of car-buying dollars "spent" on a car.

Finally, Andy has provided blank-cue cards to help car buyers beat the salesmen at their own game. He hopes the "student" will tear them out [or copy them] then use them during their next car salesmen encounters! Also, don't consider all car salesmen bad folk! Some are average people, like you and me, who must work [individually] at a difficult selling-job to make a living. There are lots of Andy's "students" working sales jobs, today, that may have worked briefly at some local car dealers -- on an apprenticeship. These "students" probably learned, quickly, enough verbal skills to change employment's in another sales occupation!

Getting Started:

To begin with, cue cards contain key letters where you can fill-in important negotiating information on used-car you consider worth buying. For example: When you see "A >" or "B >" or other letters with the pointing finger in the text, search for the same letters on your blank cue-cards. Once these pointing fingers have been located, just fill-in the requested information as you read through the Workshop. Here is an example of the physical/location-cue card and the selling-room cue card (See Figure 8.1).

166

```
┌─────────────────────────────────────────────────┐
│  LOCATION                          K >           │
│  (Salesman's name_____ )              │
├─────────────────────────────────────────────────┤
│  CAR B >              DEALER'S PRICE E >          │
│  Make / Model / Year                             │
│                      Dealer's List F >           │
│                        (wholesale)               │
│  Mileage C >        ┌──────────────────┐         │
│                     │ G > low book     │         │
│  Options D >        │ H > high book    │         │
│    air              └──────────────────┘         │
│    leather            YOUR BUYING-RANGE          │
│    CD Player, etc     I >        TO        < J    │
└─────────────────────────────────────────────────┘
```

LOCATION/PHYSICAL CUE CARD

FIGURE 8.1

Cue cards are the backbone to Andy's car-buying system. When you start to fill in these cue cards, it should motivate you to organize your collected car-buying info, better, before attempting negotiations with car salesmen. The cue-cards should help you pre-select quality-used cars. And later on, when you are negotiating for that car, the cuse cards should help you "control" your transaction with car salesmen, so you can capture a below-wholesale car-deal from a new-car dealer. Without these cue-cards -- your reference point of accurate info, you would have to trust car salesmen for all your figures. Are you willing to do that? I sure hope not!

Let's get started on the *seven-step workshop*, so we can help you get a great used-car at an incredibly low dealer price! Each workshop-step is in outline format, and laid-out to assist you in filling-out you cue-cards. Hopefully, you will use these cue-cards during your next car-buying "battle" with car salesman. Remember, only the prepared car-buyers win in today's competitive auto-marketplace!

STEP 1. CHOOSE A QUALITY CAR

In this section you will:

1.) Select a "wish" list of cars you think worth owning.

2.) Make a "experts" list of cars from reference sources, you think are worth owning, too.

3.) Combine these two car lists in a "priority" Shopping-Cue Card of "top" quality cars.

To begin constructing your wish-list, first, pick up several local newspapers with new and used-car ads inside. Then browse through the new-car ads with used cars for sale. The used cars you see advertised are typically in most demand with the public. Sales managers usually retain the new-car buyers' trades that appeal to the public.

Task #1. Go to the nearest public library. Enter and ask the reference-desk person for the last two or three months of Sunday newspapers. After receiving the stack of Sunday newspapers, go to each issue's new-car dealer's ad-section and review the used-car offered by major new-car dealers. Pre-select ten 3-year old cars that are advertised, and appeal to you. Make sure you choose cars within your economical means.

1.   6.

2.   7.

3.   8.

4.   9.

5.   10.

While you are still in the library and at the reference desk, ask for two famous consumer magazine reference resources: *Consumer Reports Magazine* and the *Kiplinger's Personal Financial Magazine.* Once you find their location on the bookshelf, select their most recent auto issues discussing new and used car. For example: If it's February 1996, the latest consumer magazine would be *Kiplinger's Personal Financial Magazine's* December issue, and if it's July 1996, the latest consumer magazine would be *Consumer Report's* April issue.

To continue the above-example, lets say you have the December 1996 *Consumer Reports Magazine* in front of you. With the issue, in front of you, seat down at a desk with paper and pencil, handy. In Consumer Reports, turn to the *Profiles of the 1996* article. This article lists all new cars being sold in the USA, in 1996. Then, read the editor's depreciation and predicted-reliability definitions in the first part of the article, so you understand the general nature of the information. Next, try to interpret each of the editor's meanings of depreciation and predicted-reliability values. Then spend a little time with a few car examples, so you can better understand what the editor's symbol's meaning and don't mean. Then read through each of your make and model car-choices in the article. Even though the information is general, it will help you pre-establish which of the new-car make and model are "rated" most valuable in the consumers' eye. Don't spend a lot of time on the article, just look through it and select a few make and model cars that both appeal to you and are within your economical means. Remember, you are not buying new cars, only a recent-new car with about 30,000 miles or less on it.

Task #2. From the *Profiles of the 1996 Cars* article, and after reviewing closely your car-choices' depreciation and predicted-reliability symbols listed in the article, pre-select five new-cars that the "experts" have attached their highest marks to. Be sure to document each car-choice's depreciation symbol, reliability symbol, and price range [as a new car] as listed in this article.

Make & Model	Depr. symbol	Rel. symbol	Price Range
1.			
2.			
3.			
4.			
5.			

Next in the Consumer Reports Magazine, look for the *1996 Cars Ratings* article inside, where recent versions of new make and model cars are tested, evaluated, and re-compared with past data taken earlier, on the same car. Note: If there's a check-mark, before the make and model car listed, the "experts" are recommending it for the next year.

Task #3. From the 1996 Cars Ratings article, but after reviewing the article -- in its entirety, pre-select seven cars with check-marks that are within your means at three-years old [approximately 2/3 of full-retail price].

1.

2.

3.

4.

5.

6.

7.

Finally in the same Consumer Reports Magazine, look for the *1996 Cars Reliability* article, where later make and model cars are compared, together, based on each car's collective 1993-1995 repair histories. Here the "experts" have selected only "best" used cars, based on how they stand up to consumer use and abuse. To begin selecting recently new cars, you need to pre-determine the size of car you intend to drive: Small cars, Medium cars, Large cars, Coupes, Sports cars, Luxury cars, Minivans, Pickups trucks, or Sport-utility vehicles. Once you determine the car's size, then pre-select similar sized cars to add to your shopping-list total. For example: On your shopping-list, you pre-selected a mid-size Saab 900. Then, when you reviewed the Consumer Report's charts on Saab 900, you discovered it was listed third from the bottom. After discovering this bit of bad news, you felt the Saab 900 didn't belong on your shopping-list, any longer. Unless you love Saab 900s and plan to own it, forever, you should select another used-car from the Consumer Report's recommended list to fill-in the missing car-choice. By up-grading your shopping-list selections with high resell-valued cars, you are adding potential value [quality-used cars] to your shopping-list. In other words, by replacing the low resell-valued cars with high resell-valued cars on your shopping-list, you are increasing the odds of purchasing a high valued-used car.

Task #4. From the *1996 Cars Reliability* article and after reviewing the many charts in detail, pre-select five reliable used cars the "experts" believe are worth owning.

1.

2.

3.

4.

5.

Now, compile your three shopping-lists, together, into one large list. And, be sure to cross out any recently new cars you feel, now, don't fit your needs. Of course, your list is too long to go shopping with, so you need to whittle the list down, further. To do this, fairly, we need to consult either the *N.A.D.A. Official Used Car Guide* or *Kelley Blue Book*. These used-car-pricing guides are easy to use. Here's what you need to get from either car-pricing guide: First, "age" each make and model car selected by four-years [1993], then record from either "pricing-guide" each car-choice's [1993] Retail Price, Trade-in Price, Loan Value, and M.S.P.R. (New-Car Price, with no options added) on a piece of paper.

After recording each car-choice's 1993 data, then you need to calculate each of the car-choice's four-year-depreciation factor. Here is the formula:

$$\frac{\text{Retail price}}{\text{M.S.R.P.}} \; X \; 100 = \text{Depreciation Factor at four years of "age"}$$

If any car-choice gets a four-year depreciation factor over 50 %, the car is worth considering, further. The 50% figure means one-half of the car's original-retail price remains in the car at four years of "age." Obviously, higher percent factors mean more resell-value in the car at "age" four. Or more money put back in you pocket when it comes time to resell it. The four-year depreciation factor is a stand way to measure all cars at one point in time. For most cars four years is its mid-way point of usefullness.

Task #5. Use the above formula and calculate the four-year-deprecation factors for each cars still on the shopping-list. After calculating, place only the car-choices with the highest four-year-depreciation factors at the top of your shopping-list. And, if a car-choice has a four-year-depreciation factor below 40 percent, remove it from your shopping-list, permanently. Finally, consider only the very "top" 10-15 quality used-cars on your "revised" shopping-list as potential cars worth shopping for.

1.   8.

2.   9.

3.   10.

4.   11.

5.   12.

6.   13.

7.   14.

                            15.

Before you rush out to buy one of those "top" used-cars on your shopping list, another piece of valuable information needs to be gathered, first. Savvy-buyers, whittle their used-car-shopping lists down, even further. The greater experience the savvy-buyer has at buying quality used cars, the shorter their shopping-list gets. Anyway, when completing the next step, buyers should discover some quality used cars "age" better than other quality used cars. This last task, will help you pick the "best" of the best used cars from within your *current shopping-list.*

Task #6. With your "top" shopping-list, construct a year-to-year depreciation chart on each used-car listed. Use the car-pricing guides to look up each car's yearly retail price, trade-in price, loan value, and M.S.R.P. Now, record this information on a piece of paper using this chart format. Try to get five or more years of pricing-data for each listed car.

DEPRECIATION CHART FOR "TOP" CAR CHOICES

Year	Retail	Trade-in	Loan Value	Deprec.
1997	$	$	$	$
1996	$	$	$	$
1995	$	$	$	$
1994	$	$	$	$ (1)
1993	$	$.	$	$
1992	$	$	$ (3)	$ (2)
1991	$	$	$	$

Note (1) A non-aggressive dealer's lowest-selling price on the 1994 used car of choice.

Note(2) The highest car-lot offer you can make on the 1994 car.

Note (3) The lowest car-lot offer you can make on the 1994 car.

Evaluation of Depreciation-Charts

Now, examine your filled-in depreciation-charts -- all at one time, so you can "see" which cars "hold" onto their re-sell values for the longest of time. What you are looking for are quality used cars that depreciate evenly in their fourth, fifth, sixth, even seventh years of "aging." Remember, your goal is to consume only two years of any particular car's downward devaluation [car's equity]. Therefore, your goal is to identify three-year-old cars with excellent re-sell values predicted several years into the future. In other words, by evaluating your just constructed depreciation-charts, you can pre-determine each car' future worth, for a short time. Once you identify which "top" cars hold their resell values and age "softly" into the future, you can make several economical car-choices that best fit your personal wants and needs. Therefore, if your car-choices' yearly-depreciation factors drops in similar cash reductions during its fourth, fifth, and sixth years of use this car will be an excellent car to resell after your use of it. Then, when the car reaches five years "age," two years into the future, you resell it to get back most of your original car-buying dollars. Ideally, to get your originally cash back from the Q-car -- two years later, you must have purchased it for well below dealer-wholesale -- equal to two years of car-depreciation! In other words, a car depreciates $1,500 dollars between its third and fifth years of use. To get your original invested money back you must make the dealer discount their car further in that same amount below deale-wholse. You may think it impossible to do, but "aggressive" sales managers "capture" most of their used-car stock from previous new-car buyers on a regular basis. "Aggressive" sales managers pride themselves at being able to "take" trade-ins equity [below dealer's wholesale] from their new-car buying clentele.

Now, it's time to reduce your *gathered* information onto one cue card: The shopping-cue card (See figure 8.2). Be sure to re-construct your "shopping" list by giving priority to cars that devaluate the least over the years.

YOUR CAR SELECTION   "EXPERT'S" SELECTION
MAKE / MODEL / YEAR   MAKE / MODEL / YEAR
IDENTIFY THE "TOP" CHOICE CARS ❂

1. _____   1. _____
2. _____   2. _____
3. _____   3. _____
4. _____   4. _____
5. _____   5. _____

SHOPPING-CUE CARD
FIGURE 8.2

STEP 2. LOCATING QUALITY CARS

In this section you will:

1.) Be given some car-shopping rules, to assist you.

2.) Locate quality used-cars from your shopping-cue card

3.) Test driving "top" car-choices at local car dealerships

As stated earlier, encountering car salesmen is dangerous business for "unprepared" car buyers. Therefore, a few car-shopping strategies are appropriate, at this time, to "protect" the beginning car shopper from "aggressive" car salesmen.

- Indicate to the car salesmen, you're in the market to buy a car, today!

- Don't negotiate or haggle over any car on the car lot.

- Locate and test drive <u>cars</u> listed on shopping-cue card.

- If no salesman will spend time with you, ask for the Fleet-Sales Manager, and he will help you or assign another car salesman to assist you, further.

Well, it's time to get your feet "wet" visiting a few new-car dealers. Don't forget your shopping-cue card, though, so you can scan each dealer's car-lot inventory for cars on your listed, quickly. In many cases, car salesmen will attemp to select a car for you. Avoid changing the make/model/year of any cars you've shopping for. Just stick to your simple shopping plan; locate and test drive quality used-cars that hold their resell values the longest of time!

Once you do locate a car-choice, make sure to collect the additional information needed to fill-in your next cue-card called, "location/physical cue card." In most cases, doing this is not advised in front of car salesmen. Therefore, a piece of paper or the back of the salesman's business card will do just as well. But for the purposes of this book, the location/physical cue card's in your hands, now. And this is what you need to record on it, during your shopping-phase:

A >   The location of the car
B >   The Make/Model/Year of car
C >   The mileage on the car
D >   The factory-installed options in the car
E >   The dealer's price for the car

Remember, the letters with the arrows attached to them have specific locations to record information at, within the cue-card system. Probably, the salesman's business card is the best place to initially record the A> to E> information on (See figure 8.3 for example of back side L/P cue card).

CAR-SHOPPING 'ET' LIST

A > location of dealer-car

B > the make/model/year

C > the car's mileage

D > the factory-option

E > the dealer's asking price

Get salesman's business card

Give dealer's car test drive.

Does it look like a brand new?

TEST-DRIVE QUICK CHECK LIST

	YES	NO
First impression of car	——	——
Exterior is free of dents	——	——
Interior: Seat not lumpy	——	——
look under floor mats	——	——
Wear on brake pedal	——	——
Armrest driver's side	——	——
Engine Compartment everything is in place	——	——
No visable damage	——	——
Brakes work fine	——	——
Drives straight on road	——	——
No visable exhaust fume	——	——
Last impression of car	——	——

NEVER SHOP IN THE NIGHT

LOCATION/PHYSICAL CUE CARD
BACKSIDE FIGURE 8.3

177

Inspecting the car:

When you locate a "top" ten used-car from your shopping-cue card, the next step is to give it a thorough test drive. Before getting in and test driving it, though, give it a "walk around" inspection to make sure it still appeals to you. The general ideal of walking around the car is to "see" if the car's exterior "glows" -- as it did when it was brand new, and if the car's interior "smells" -- like it did when new. If your answer, to both these quick inspections is yes it looks new, only then consider giving it a test drive (See Appendix B for more details on examining a used car's vital parts).

The warm up:

Once inside the car, turn all the knobs and switches to make sure everything works electrically in the car. Turn the motor on and let the engine warm up. If anything is wrong, make its correction part of the contract. If the car passes all these two quick inspections, then take it out for a test drive. Once you are on the road, the car's power and handling are two features worth noting. If the car is weak or handles poorly when you turn it, make a note of it on your cue-card. Also, check the car's roof height, in regards to the driver's head. If any part of your hair touches it, this car is not for you. The worst thing you could do is buy a car that don't fit you, comfortably. Test drive the car-of choice for more than fifteen minutes.

The final step to evaluating a car is to leave the dealership, after the test drive! Yes, leave the car lot without making any offers or chatting with the car salesman you're with. Just remind him, though, as you're leaving the lot, if you decide to buy his car, you may make an appointment with him, later. Remember, you are trying to locate several "cream puff" used cars. You don't have time to negotiate with any of the car salesmen, yet. Merely ask for each car salesman's business card -- if you have not already, and leave the car lot, pronto!

178

STEP 3. DESIGN YOUR DEAL

In this section you will:

1.) Complete your cue-cards on the "top" used-cars you have located at several new-car dealerships.

2.) Determine your car-lot offers and buying-ranges on the "top" used-cars you feel are worth owning.

You should have five to ten "top" used-cars you are very interested in owning. By now, you know where each "top" car-of choice is located and many details about each car's condition. You know the salesman's name at each dealer-car location. But before you can effectively negotiate for any "top" car-of choice, you need to know what the dealer paid for them. How can you determine that, accurately? To begin with, you can't know, exactly, what someone else paid for a car. The best you can do is "guess" at what they paid for them. After making your "guess" on what the dealer paid for the car, you need to consider how much profit to pay them, too. Finally, when you do determine what the dealer paid for the car and what amount to pay the dealer, you need to place this information on the location/physical cue card for each of the "top" cars. To accomplish this, we need to visit the library one last time.

Once you are in the library and at the reference desk, ask for their copy of the *N.A.D.A. Official Used Car Guide or the Kelley Blue Book.* Either pricing-guide will be okay for your researching needs. With one of these pricing guides, in front of you, a calculator, pencil, paper, you are now ready to complete each of your location/physical cue cards. First, take out several blank location/physical cue cards and identify each car-of choice's car-lot data off the car salesman's business cards and/or pieces of paper. Transfer this car-lot data, correctly, on each L/p cue-card: A > location of "top" used car; B > make & model & year of "top" used car; C > mileage; D > options; E > dealer's asking price, and include the first car salesman's name (See figure 8.4).

```
┌─────────────────────────────────────────────────────┐
│  LOCATION A                          K >             │
│  (Salesman's name_____ )          │
├─────────────────────────────────────────────────────┤
│  CAR B >                  DEALER'S PRICE E >          │
│  Make/ Model/ Year                                   │
│                           Dealer's List F >          │
│                           (wholesale)                │
│  Mileage C >             ┌─────────────────────────┐ │
│                          │ G > low book            │ │
│  Options D >             │ H > high book           │ │
│     air                  └─────────────────────────┘ │
│     leather               YOUR BUYING-RANGE          │
│     CD Player, etc        I >      TO          < J   │
└─────────────────────────────────────────────────────┘
```

LOCATION/PHYSICAL CUE CARD
FIGURE 8.4

Now, with your location/physical cue cards looking a bit more useful, at this point, you need to make your "guess" at what these car dealer's paid for each of the "top" used cars. To make a "guess" on a "top" used-car, accurately, you need to locate the year/make/model of the car, in question, inside one of the pricing-guides. So, if your "top" car is three-years old, "age" it two years more and mark down its five-year old wholesale-value at the location/physical cue card's buying-range I >. Keep in mind, though, if the new-car dealer's sales manager isn't the "aggressive" sales type or the new-car dealership is very small, your "guess" will be considered too low to both of them. Remember, it's the low-end of your buying-range I > < J. To figure out the high-end of your buying-range, just add what you think the dealer's profit should be for selling you their used-car. If you think the dealer's profit should be $500, then < J equals I > plus $500. If the dealer's sales manager is of the "aggressive" type, the I > < J numbers will be close, enough!

180

Before closing your pricing-guide, write down the car's true retail price at G > **Figure**; then take that G > **figure** and add any major factory-installed options (at their wholesale values listed in the pricing guide) to get the H > **Figure**. Also, to get the F > **Figure** on the car, you need to record the M.S.R.P or dealer list price when new [without options being added, yet. Finally, record your trade-in's wholesale-value listed in the pricing-guide [look up make/model/year of car] and place that value at K > **Figure**.

Summary:

By this time, you have all the "vital" data needed to make a deal for a quality used-car from your shopping-cue card. More important, you have in your possession, the "similar" pricing-figures car salesmen have when selling consumer's used cars. Now, if the salesmen attempt to give you extra-low numbers on your trade-in, for example, you will know it immediately by simply glancing at your cue cards. Or if car salesmen quote you high "selling" prices for their cars for sale [your car-choice], you will know immediately how far from your buying-range they are. You're in a much "better" negotiating-position than the car salesmen are, even though they don't know it.

STEP 4. PRACTICE MAKES PERFECT

In this section you will:

1.) A short course at using your cue cards

2.) Practice with your cue-cards by "working" the sellers at the bottom of your car-shopping list

3.) Build-up your "buyer's" confidence inside the dealer-selling office, by having a few practice runs

Up to this point, you've only been gathering data on used cars and placing the information on various cue-cards. Soon, you will be buying the "top" used car-of choice for real. But first, you should try to get some "practice runs" under your belt, to help you understand the basic "exchanges" of normal car-bargaining. You don't want to encounter car salesmen for "real," when the stakes are your money, so a few "practice runs" seem a "logical" next step for the beginning negotiator.

The first "practice run:"

To begin your "practice-runs," get your location/physical cue cards, together, and review which two or three "top" car-choices you consider not worth negotiating further on. After you have made your choices, pull their L/P cue cards to identify the salesmen you will be practicing with. Then make arrangements to meet he/she at their car-dealership. for your "practice-runs." Before meeting, though, be sure your selling-room cue cards have been updated, and all the requested information has been transferred to their correct selling-room cue card locations: trade-in value at K > , car-lot offer at I >, the planned down-payment amount at M >, and the monthly payments figures at N > (See Appendix A for the monthly-payment's calculator).

Since you have done one set of calculations in chapter three, making further calculations and transfers onto selling-room cue cards should be easier, now! Remember, selling-room cue cards are your "center-of-reference" inside the salesman's office. Make sure you bring a pencil along to fill-in any revised-pricing data onto the cue cards during negotiations! Caution: The selling-room cue-card contains your negotiating facts and figures on a specific dealer-car you're considering to buy from the dealership. Don't leave your cue-cards -- unattended, you may be surprised to discover they're missing, later on. The selling-room cue card is the single most "powerful" cue card in your hands. Most car salesmen "fear" informed car buyers, so use your cue-cards, cautiously (See figure 8.5).

```
TRADE: K >
  (WHOLESALE VALUE L >            )

PRICE OF CAR: I >


DOWN: M >


MONTHLY: N >
```

SELLING-ROOM CUE CARD
FIGURE 8.5

Besides taking your cue cards with you, you might consider bringing along additional "weapons," before meeting a car salesman.

- A "sidekick" friend, if you are alone. Remember, a "sidekick's" job is to keep the salesmen off balance, during your negotiations with the sales manager.

- Take some petty-cash with you (not during the practice-runs). Remember, this petty-cash is the only cash you give, anyone, inside the dealer's selling room, until after the contract is signed. Whatever amount you plan to release -- ten, twenty, or fifty dollars, don't let any salesman hold you "hostage" because of it -- by not returning it to you. Request your cash back and then just leave the car dealership. When you have left the dealer's property, report both the car salesman's name and the dealer's location to a local Department of Motor Vehicle's Official. They will look into the matter for you, and you will get your petty-cash back, pronto!

- An extra set of car keys (Don't release keys to anyone during the practice-run. If you do, you could be held "hostage.")

  Author's note: If you have released your keys to a salesman, and you want to leave the dealer. Tell the salesman you will call the police for not returning your car keys to you, pronto. If the salesman still fails to respond to your car-keys request, just leave the car dealership and then call the police!

- A calculator, pen and extra paper

- Business cards of the car salesmen you've already met, during your car-shopping phase

The First "Practice-Run" Begins:

When you get to the dealer-car's location, try to contact the same salesman you had met, earlier. Make sure the same used-car is for sale and in the used-car lot. Take another look at it [don't test drive it]. Remember, during your two "practice-runs," you must look like "today-buyers" to these salesmen, so they stay with you throughout the "practice-runs." Use words that may indicate an urgency to buy the car, today! At this point, though, you don't want to be over "acting" or too demanding with these salesmen. The idea of "practicing" with car salesmen is to learn how to "flow" with their selling-tactics, sales ploys and consume their selling-time with small talk -- of your own. There's plenty of time, later on, to take *control* over them, inside their selling-rooms.

Another idea of "practicing" on car salesmen, is to witness their "verbal" selling-games when inside the selling-room! Once inside the selling-room, your "acting" skills will need to believable to the salesmen. In other words, if you don't look or act sincere with car salesmen, they will label you as a "fake" buyer or "looker," and throw you off the car-lot.

Car salesman aren't impressed with actors, they prefer the sincere car buyer to sell to. Anyway, after you "practice" with a few salesmen, you will begin to be more "aware" of their ways -- the way they think and talk. It's important to improve your "acting skills" with car salesmen, so you can compete with "aggressive" sellers and capture a great price.

By presenting your car-lot offer to the salesmen, they are trained to "walk" you into the selling-room. Meanwhile, the salesmen pre-plan their "future moves" the remaining time they are with you. Before they start negotiating with you, they must begin their acting-skills as a newly found friend. In other words, all car salesmen's must try to become a "trusting" friend of the buyer, before "walking" them to a selling-room.

In the Selling Room:

When you begin negotiating with salesmen, they may demand up-front cash to hold you "hostage" in the selling room. Avoid releasing any money to them, during your "practice-runs." The salesmen may become suspicious of your buying-motives, though, when you don't give them money. If this happens, change the topic or ask a questions! If your salesman continues demanding money or keys from you -- as a sign of good faith, tell him; "It's too early to release my cash, yet!"

During negotiations, the car salesman will dominate most of the proceedings. Attempt "interfering" with the salesman's chattering. Learn how to interfere with the salesman's negotiations, by asking questions related only to the four sections of your selling-room cue card: Trade-n Price; Price of Car; Down-Payment, and Monthly-Payments. Change the conversation's direction within the above four sections at every possible opportunity. Look at your cue-cards, and then make a counter-offer that benefits you. When the salesman demands additional down-payment cash, look at your cue-cards, and then make a counter-offer that benefits you. When the salesman quotes you high monthly-payments, look at your cue-cards, and then make a counter-offer with much lower monthly-payments. Note: In regards to monthly payments, try to maneuver the salesman, by "acting" overly concerned with the monthly-payments amount. "Aggressive" car buyers learn how to consume most of a car salesman's selling-time, by talking monthly-payment figures with him. Say anything that is "believable" to car salesmen, so they are willing to spend extra time on you to sell you a car, now.

After you develop a few car-buying "tactics" of your own, change your negotiating direction to see if the car salesman is listening to you. By changing the topic with the salesman, often, you "teach" the salesman to listen to your small talk or serious negotiating terms more closely. Once you believe the salesman is listen to you, manuuver the car salesman around the negotiating-table by talking: Trade-in Price, Price of Car, month-Payment, and down-payment amounts. The reason for taking time to "learn" a few car buying "tactics" is balance the negotiating-table better. When both parties can know the rules and can compete with each other, equally, they will make better agreements with each other [money for goods]. In other words, consumer with money should respect their advantage, over persons with goods [cars] while negotiating a fair exchange with each other.

Of course, the very best buying "tactic" for a savvy-buyer's to learn is being able to "waste-away" the salesman's selling-time. One favorite "tactic" to waste away a salesman's selling time is to fabricate a family "fight" in front of them! In other words, customers who are "fighting with each other can't be sold anything, in the moment. The result is car salesmen remain "helpless," during the family spat and additional selling-time is further "wasted-away." Another favorite "tactic" is to leave your seating position and walk around the selling/closing-room and/or leave the salesman's office to select another car. If the car salesman gives up on you and "turns-you-over" to a second salesman practice on him/her for a bit longer, too. If the "second" car salesman can recognize your "militant" buying-tactics, he/she will try to regain "control" over you and the deal. If this happens earlier in the negotiations, you will learn no more with your "practice-run." Therefore, you should pick up your things, stand up, and while walking to your car thank everybody for their time spent. Don't stop walking to your car, either, just leave the dealership for your next "practice-run" appointment.

Car salesmen may use any manner of selling "tricks" to confuse and confound car buyers to sell them cars. Try to "study" their selling "tactics," during the "practice-runs." Put yourself in the salesmen's shoes, as the deal making progresses. Try to "see" their reasoning for asking you a question or demanding cash from you. Here are a few selling "tricks" salesmen use on unwary consumers:

- The Hand-Off (giving you to another salesman, not always a closer)
- The Cross-Over (changing to another element on the salesman's worksheet)
- The Imaginary-Offer ("If we could ___, would you buy today?)
- The Questions-Ploy (The salesman answers your question with another question to make things even more confusing)
- The Pity-Ploy ("My boss will fire me if I bring him your offer as is, lets change it to _____ .)

Don't get upset, though, when you recognize car salesmen using any of these selling "tactics." Salesmen rarely get "personal" with anyone -- it's just business as usual with them. Just, enjoy the salesman's "acting" creativeness on the job. You can stop all these car salesmen selling "tricks" when you use cue-cards against them.

Use Your Cue Cards:

After a few "practice-runs" under your belt, you will begin to understand the value of your cue-cards and their "control" over both you and the salesmen. Try to review your cue-cards discretely, at first, when negotiating inside the dealer's selling-room. Let your negotiations proceed, for a while, before you begin to show-off your cue-cards. As your deal-making continues its normal conclusion with both the car salesman and closer-boss, reveal your cue-cards more often with them. When your deal-making comes to its "natural" conclusion reveal your cue-cards, continually. And, then re-confirm all your agreed-upon figures, before you sign on the dotted line, no exceptions.

Cue-cards are important because:

- They slow down or stop the car salesman's selling progress

- They keep tabs of the customer's "numbers" in their deal

- They can re-start negotiations, at any point, when you wish to proceed

- They are your "center-of-reference," inside the selling-room. Without your cue-cards, you would lose "control" of the deal-making process.

Summing Up:

Remember, your "practice-runs" are supposed to give you the necessary experience to maneuver car salesmen when you wish to. These "practice-runs" enable you to learn a few "buying "tricks" of your own. You don't want to buy any of these cars or get too involved with any of the car salesmen. You just want to "practice" with them, a little, so you can develop into a savvy-buyer like Joan or Andy Smith. When you feel you've learned enough with these car salesmen stop your "practice-runs." That's right, the last lesson to learn is to head for the dealership's door! Of all the signals you can send car salesmen, walking out is the clearest and most powerful buyer-weapon you can possess!

5. PLAYING FOR REAL

In this section you will:

1.) Test drive the "top" used-car <u>again</u> and re-verify its cue-card data is correct

2.) After making the car-lot offer, "walk" the salesman to his office, and then begin your negotiations with the cue-cards at your side

By now you have completed several "practice-runs" with car salesmen. Possibly you are making plans to buy the car you really want. With your "exposure to salesmen" over, your "control" over them is more likely. Since, you've "studied" the basic negotiations' salesmen use, you feel it's more difficult for them to confuse or confound you, any further. If this is true, you're ready to take charge of your life and "take" your fair-deal from a car salesman.

Author's note: If you continue to get ditched, just ask for the Fleet-Sales Manager. The fleet-sales manager <u>must</u> re-assign you to another car salesman. Remember he works for the sales manager. All "aggressive" sales managers believe their customers are too important to lose. In most cases, the fleet-sales manager will delegate a new-car salesman to you. That is just what you want!

<u>Updating Your Cue-Cards:</u>

Be discreet when you update your cue cards in front of car salesmen. Sometimes, "sidekicks" have a better seating position inside the salesman's office, and help you make the necessary changes on your cue-cards. If not, at least your "sidekick" can hold onto them in-between updating periods. Be secretive with your changes, early on, in your deal-making efforts. Later on, you can be less secretive with car salesmen, as the deal-making comes to a near close.

This accomplishes several things:

- This shows the car salesmen/closers you are recording their figures quoted to you

- Cue-cards help you keep track of the all figures quoted to the car salesmen/closers

- The car salesmen/closers don't know what to expect next from you or your cue-cards

Consuming Selling-Time With Dealer Financing:

Often, car salesmen and their closers confuse and confound their customers during the monthly-payment chatter on the dealer's 4-step worksheet. Car salesmen/closers "throw" confusing monthly-payments figures, in front of customers, to imply they have "won" an excellent deal from the dealer. The monthly-payments chatter can work both ways, though! When the car-buyers say "yes" to dealer financing, they say "yes" to another way of taking away "vital" sales-time with car salesmen. In fact, this is the best way to consume two-hours of their time with them, is to act as a monthly payment buyer would -- concerned with their payments. Then, just before the contract gets written up, they change back to a cash-buyers -- concerned with the car's selling price and/or their trade-in dollars. Savvy-buyers understand they must "act" just like other consumers do, "fool" car salesmen, closers and their sales managers into wasting valuable selling-time on them. Even so, you must pre-arrange your own "outside" financing, ahead of time!

Dealerships make extra money when they offer loans to car buyers at ridiculously high-interest rates. If the buyer asks the dealer to assist them in financing the car, the salesman/closer and sales manager are eager to close a deal.

Often, sales managers will accept minimum-profit deals [thin deals] on their used-cars, if they can offset them with extra money earned, elsewhere. In other words, by "pushing" the customer's financing arrangements to local finance companies, the dealer's sales manager can earn extra cash. Savvy-buyers know dealers make extra cash "pushing" their customer's car-deals into local finance companies. Most savvy-buyers want to avoid this extra-cash loss, so they make outside financing arrangements with a bank or credit union, beforehand. Also, they avoid telling any of the dealer's salesmen or closers, because this information could reduce their chances of closing a "thin deal" with the dealer's sales manager. After the contract is signed and car is delivered the savvy-buyer, they return to the dealer the very next working day, and pay-off the remaining car-debt owed on the car. The results are obvious: The dealer's "thin deal," just got thinner!

Summing Up:

For savvy-buyers, the critical figures on the salesmen's 4-step worksheet are: down payment, price of car, and trade-in dollars. It's not difficult for savvy-buyers to keep tabs on these three figures when they are using their cue-cards. For the dealer's sales manager, though, the customer's monthly-payments and trade-in amounts are the two "best" areas to confuse or confound them on the 4-step worksheet. To begin confusing the customer, the sales manager must "trick" them into "believing" they received extra trade-in cash, free! To continue the confusing customers, the sales manager must "trick" them, even further, into "believing" they received "discounts" in the form of lower monthly payments. In both of these cases, "crafty" sales managers make their car-buying clientele "feel" they got something for nothing! Cue-cards stop these "illusions" made by sales managers from ever developing. I guess the goal of "aggressive" salesmen and gift of gab or verbal chattering is to impact the car-buyer's pocketbook! Cue-cards help car buyers stay focused on the more important buying-figures of their car-deal.

6. FORCING AN AGREEMENT

In this section you will:

1.) Restate your final offer, then attempt to close the deal, in your favor

2.) Force an agreement to happen, now, or slowly "walk" off the dealer's car lot

If you have turned the car-deal, in your favor, it's time to close it -- in the form of a written contract. When you feel you are within your <u>buying-range</u> or you have "pushed" the sales team far enough, then it's time to reach an agreement. If the car-deal's not, in your favor, then it's time to leave the car dealership and start over, elsewhere.

<u>When the Deal Gets Stuck:</u>

One way to "push" an agreement to its close is to begin asking the car salesmen "If I ____, will you agree" statements. Of course, they will recognize you're trying to "push" the deal forward. Even so, they should proceed with the negotiations, because they have much time "invested" in you by, now. To "jump start" their negotiations, again, look at your selling-room cue-card, for a category you still can remain vague at, and agree with the salesman. Of course, the car salesmen expects more than your vague promises before they present their signed contract to you. If you fail to get a ready-to-sign agreement presented to you, after several "jump start" attempts, maybe you need to take much stronger action with the salesmen, before you prematurely leave for good!

<u>Walking out "shock" treatment:</u>

When all else fails and/or you feel you've pushed the salesmen the limit, pull out your cue cards and repeat your "last" offer, one more time! Then, quickly, stand up and walk out of the salesman's office towards your car. Don't walk quickly, though, and don't look back, either! Before you reach your car, the salesmen may whistle you back and say, "Okay, you have won <u>or</u> We'll take your last-offer, now." Sometimes, it takes a kind of "bullying" of the car salesmen to get them to bend your way, in the end. Don't feel sorry for them, either, or you may fall victim of yet another one of their self-pity selling "ploys."

As the negotiations come to a close, it's important to take your selling-room cue card, and write in the latest terms of the deal, before you shake on it. If you write the final terms on your cue-cards and car salesmen "see" this happening, they should not change your figures on the final contract.

Caution: If you have a trade-in, as part of the deal and you plan to take it out of the deal, it's time to pull it out -- before you do any hand shaking with the closer or F/I Manager! You can do this by "acting" upset for having to "walk out" to get your fair deal. Any excuse will do! But do take your trade-in out in the last moments of the deal. Sometimes, closers try and alter the agreed-upon deal, anyway, because you've changed it, first. Just remember you have the upper-hand, at the moment, by simply walking out of the deal, again, if you don't get your fair deal!

Summing Up:

When car salesmen spend their selling-time with customers, they think of only one thing: Get the deal signed and then count the profits "taken." In other words, the sales manager, closer and car salesmen have made all "attempts" possible to "take" profit from you, and it's time to sign you to a contract and count their sales commissions. When savvy-buyers buy cars from car salesmen, they want to put their invested-money into a high resell valued car and not the salesmen's pockets. They know used-cars are a means of saving money [on wheels] while driving them at the same time. But before they sign any contract, they must review it, first.

7. REVIEWING THE CONTRACT

In this section you will:

1.) Review the contract

2.) Resolve any problems found in the contract, before signing it

3.) Drive off in your recently-new car

Sometimes, "Aggressive" sales managers assign their "best" profit-taker as their Finance & Insurance Manager. It will be a closer or manager-level person assigned the important task of making-ready the final contracts. Also, remember, nothing is agreed-upon, until it's in writing and both you and the sales manager have signed on the dotted lines.

Contract "Tricks:"

The F/I manager probably will mention to the car buyer, they don't need to read the contract and that everything agreed-upon is written into the contract. Don't believe him! Also, the F/I manager may try to speed things up, during the contract review session. Refuse to be rushed! Don't sign anything, until you understand it, clearly! If the F/I manager requests you to sign the trade-in's ownership-papers before signing the final contract, you may lose your trade-in and even leave the dealership without either car. For example: You signed-over your trade's ownership paper to the dealership and a contract fails to happen for you. By signing-over your trade's ownership paper, the dealership is now the "rightful" owner to your trade-in, and not you! And, if you are asked to leave the dealership, you will find your car is missing because the dealer's taken possession of it. Of course, they will send you a check, later on!

In most cases the closer or F/I manager will "talk" you through all the necessary paperwork to complete the contract. He will state the purpose of each document and then ask you to sign in several places. Make sure you know what each document is, before signing. Even take it -- in your hands and read it, before signing it. Be particularly careful, and check to make sure:

- No extras are added, like extended warranties and detailing services (most are worthless)
- All the figures are correct and in the right place (check your cue cards)
- That dealer financing allows early loan pay-off without penalty
- That the D.M.V. license fees are correct (Sometimes salesmen inflate these figures, earlier in the deal, then take that difference in the form of another profit.)
- That all selling-room promises are recorded in the amendments section of your contract

When the contract's figures are incorrect, first, review your cue-card data and then repeat the correct figures to the F/I manager. You must get the incorrect figures changed, before signing the contract! Insist that your contract be changed, i.e., rewritten! Don't be bullied or intimidated by any F/I manager. Remember, they have substantial time invested in you and their deal! If the F/I manager loses you to another dealer because you walked out of the deal, he will have to answer to the sales manager for the loss.

Taking Possession of the Car:

All your hard work is about to pay off as you prepare to drive away in your quality used-car. Here are two more things to think about, before you drive off the car-lot.

Never take possession of the car until:

- The sales manager has signed the contract and given you a copy on it.

- You have signed the contract, after releasing the down-payment check or cash to the F/I manager. If you have given, earlier, some petty-cash, get a receipt for it or make them return the cash.
- You have "outside" financing available to you, so you can change the signed-contract's financial agreement with the dealership the next working day.

Looking Ahead:

I hope the seven-step "workshop" has helped you to become a savvy-buyer, yourself. Car salesmen come in many shapes and sizes, but all like to convert a shopper into a today-buyer. When salesmen encounter savvy-buyers, they feel most grateful of the sale and even extend a shaking hand to them for their ability to compete with the sales team.

9
The Radio Interview

Hey, there! This is Tony Talken. It's two o'clock and time for the K.A.R.S. Consumer corner! Today we have with us Mr. Darrell Parrish, a former car salesman and author of three popular car buying/leasing books: The Car Buyer's Art, Used Cars and Lease Cars.

"Now, we've all had our own experiences at buying a car, so let's listen to a teacher in the art of car buying."

"Remember, the number to call is 555-8585 or, outside the 243 area code, call (800) XXX-XXXX. Lets hear from you, because are why we're here. But, first a word from the people who pay the bills, our sponsors."

"Okay, we're back! So you think you're ready to buy a car. You heard about the sting, the scam, and the flim-flam; Now let us fill you in on the verbal "bait and switch" scam. By skimming a bit here and a bit there, the "professional" car salesmen, work together, to take the average car buyer for a ride, in more senses than one. Like a lamb to the slaughter, the buyer is lead through a sequence of selling-steps designed to relieve them of their hard earned money, in exchange for a new or used car, they may not even want!"

"We're talking with Darrell Parrish, author of several car buying books in bookstores, everywhere."

TONY: Darrell, it appears to me, on the surface, your books look more like "how-to-get-even" type literature!

DARRELL: My Books' goal is to decipher the car dealer's tangling-webs for all to see. For example: When I assert sales managers are the real "villains," and not the car salesmen they hire to work at the dealers, I attempt to "prove" it in my books. When I indicate some sales managers "bait and switch" their customers, I mean they train their sales teams to "bait" the customer with lots of car-lot offers, then "switch" them to what it really takes to buy the new or used car.

TONY: Sounds like strong medicine to me, Darrell. I didn't think car salesmen are so bad of people.

DARRELL: Individually, car salesmen are harmless, but when they "work" on a customer, together, they can be overwhelming and eventually move the negotiations in the favor of the dealership.

TONY: You mentioned your car buying course was popular at California State University at Long Beach. Are you still teaching there?

DARRELL: No. Presently, I teach over radio, like I'm doing here. The college course was only one unit or 15-hours of instruction. I taught there for three years. It helped me shape my first book: The Car Buyer's Art. The students were allowed to "attack" the course's materials. It was a good experience for me.

TONY: Why is car buying so difficult and, for many of us, so painful?

DARRELL: I believe dealers want it that way! If their sales teams can confuse and confound the customers, additional dealer-profits are possible. Car salesmen have two ways to confuse and confound customers: verbally and on paper. First, when car salesmen encounter their customers, and second, when they try to sell their customers on paper -- eventually getting them to sign it.

TONY: You mean car salesmen complicate a customer's decision-making so they make a mistake.

DARRELL: Yes! I think this is all done on purpose, so car buyers make enough mistakes, they benefit the dealer when it comes time to sign on the dotted line.

TONY: I think the local car dealers are going to get upset with this interview. Are all your interviews the same?

DARRELL: I think there is a need to reveal the salesmen's selling-secrets. I've been on over 1,000 radio interviews, most local dealers hate their selling "tactics" released to the public. You may get a few dealer's to call in, Tony!

TONY: I bet! Look in the other room. Our sales manager is with several dealers and their lawyers.

DARRELL: Don't worry. I only wish to teach the public how to win at the car buying process.

TONY: Outside of a house, the car is the biggest item a person or family will purchase.

DARRELL: I wonder. When you consider the number of cars a family buys in thirty years. And you combine that figure with the total interest paid on all those vehicles, you will come up with a sizable total figure. A figure twice the size of an average house, in my opinion!

TONY: What are some of the unnecessary risks car buyer expose themselves to when buying a car?

DARRELL: I think when customers buy new or lease their new cars, they have made a serious mistake.

TONY: Why is buying or leasing new cars a mistake?

DARRELL: The total devaluation a new car experiences in its fist four years is often half the car's total worth. In other words, for consumers to drive

	new car, or lease cars for that matter, they must lose half their car's resell worth -- if they sold their cars at four years of "age." When you buy a used car, you lose little out-of-pocket cash, during ownership.
TONY:	You mean I can own a used car, for free!
DARRELL:	No. Not exactly! The entire purpose of Used Cars is to teach consumers how to search for and buy quality used cars, but well below dealer's wholesale. Then after driving them, two years on the road, resell them back to private parties for much higher prices than what was originally paid for them.
TONY:	Sounds like a dream.
DARRELL:	Ex-car salesmen do it all the time. You don't think they would put their hard-earned money in a new car! That's wasting money, in my opinion.
TONY:	So deprecation is one un-necessary risk. Are their others?
DARRELL:	Buying the wrong car. If consumers fail to do any research on which car's are worth owning, they will most likly chose the wrong car!
TONY:	If I can't decide between a sports car and 4 by 4, will your Used Cars book help me select one?
DARRELL:	After reviewing a couple consumer magazines and used-car-pricing guides, The reader is given a simple formula to help pre-select which used cars are worth investing in.
TONY:	There are lots of used cars to choose from. But, which ones are worth really investing in?
DARRELL:	Any used car that retains over 50% of its original retail price, after four years of use.

"Lets take a break for our sponsors, folks." Tony was last seen talking with the advertising manager and several radio-station lawyers. It appears several car dealers are upset with the way the interview is progressing. Tony and Darrell have a used-car dealer setting in on the show, today.

202

TONY: We're back folks! Johnny, station manager has asked several car dealers to listen in on our program. A owner of Friendly Freddy's Used Car lot is now setting in with us! Thanks for coming Freddy.

FREDDY: I'm doing just fine, thank you.

TONY: How are we doing? I mean how's Darrell doing?

FREDDY: Not good. I fail to see why you let such a rat-fink of a guy get on the aire.

TONY: I don't think Darrell is the ratting type. He's been on more than 150 television stations and 1,000 radio interviews as a consumer advocate. What's wrong with helping consumers, anyway?

FREDDY: I've read his books. He lies alot in them. He hates car salesmen, that all!

TONY: Darrell, do you hate car salesmen.

DARRELL: Not at all. I dislike "aggressive" sales managers who take excessive amounts of money from unwary consumers.

FREDDY: In Used Cars, Mr. Parrish indicates never shop at used-car dealers. Well, I'm a used car dealer! I do a lot advertising here on this station. Either he leaves the interview or I will not spend another advertising dollar here!

Everyone is silent, even the salesman for a change. Tony takes a quick station break and leaves the room. Darrell and Freddy are left alone. Here's what transpired in jus a few minutes.

FREDDY: I've been trying to get on the aire with you for the last ten years. Now's my chance to show you!

DARRELL: Show me what? Fred, I've been teaching these car-buyng principles to radio audiences for the last 16-years, now. What could you possible show me?

FREDDY: I brought my attorneys. thay are taping ever word you say. They promised me, I could sue you when you make a mistake!

DARRELL: Do you think you are the only one who's tried to sue me! Look! As long as I remain a teacher -- give basic car buying strategies to the public, the law of the land will protect my right to speak out. That is exactly what I've been doing!

FREDDY: I'll get the last laugh, mister! You are a bastard.

Tony has re-entered the studio and is displeased with Freddy's last comment. He sit down at the control panel and pulls out the last commercial. The general manager enters to ask Fred to leave.

TONY: We're back folks. Freddy had to leave for a moment. Darrell, can you stay with us, and answer some questions from the audience?

DARRELL: Thanks for asking. Usually, when an interview progresses in this manner, other dealers will try to interrupt it.

TONY: Don't worry about that. Our station manager has instructed us to continue. He believes helping the consumer win in the marketplace is news worth learning for us all. Well the telephone is jammed. Lets chat with a few of our callers, now!

CALLER 1: My husband works as a car salesman. We think car salesmen have the worst end of the stick. Jim works 60 hours a week, I never get to see him, these days. Your guest makes my husband job harder.

We're off the air Mr. Parish! I guess we have a lot of car dealers in the area. I have never had this happen to me before. I've interviewed many strange guys, and you don't fit their M.O. I'm very sorry for consuming your time! Tony what's important is I've been of some help to your car-buying listeners. Thanks for having on your program.

10
We Help At CCCS

Author's Note: I have requested this organization to present their consumer views on buying cars, used, and possible financial-impacts on the American family. I hope you find the information useful, both before and after your next car purchase. Also, if you get into some trouble, after your car purchase, CCCS personnel can be of service to you. The CCCS organization is nationally recognized and they have much clout with many in the business community. To my readers, I release their presentation in its entirety, authored by Mr. Richard Pittman, Director, of Consumer Credit Counseling Service of Los Angeles.

With the enclosed information in this chapter, we hope you will enter the marketplace with greater confidence. If you get into trouble with your car purchase we hope the enclosed data will assist you before and after the sale.

Consider this a final exam to be sure you are ready not only for the exhilaration of a victorious hunt, but also that you will survive financially with the decisions you are about to make. Good Hunting!

Some have estimated 30 million used cars will be sold in the United States during 1997; almost twice the number of expected new-car sales.

Buying a car has been said to be among the most nerve-racking experiences imaginable, yet most of us live a life of mobility, requiring a dependable, and affordable vehicle.

A simple test to start. . . . . . .

Was your last used car experience:

(a) An opportunity to inherit the problems of the previous owner (Replacing one set of repair bills for another)?

(b) An opportunity to be separated from your hard earned money?

(c) A rewarding opportunity to put your knowledge and skills [about car repairs] to work?

(d) "I never bought a car before, and I'm worried [sick] based on horror stories heard from others."

What your answers could mean, if you chose:

(a) You are looking to gain power over your car purchases. Would a professional inspection of the car made a difference?

(b) You may still be kicking yourself for paying too much for a prior car purchase, but are determined not to repeat the same mistake next time.

(c) You are happy, but may be unsure if this feeling [of being happy] is based on:

1. True awareness

2. Some degree of "ignorance is bliss."

Or, do you want to work to improve your results [at car buying] even more next time?

(d) Ah, a car-buyer trainee! Remember when you first learned to drive? It required a fair amount of practice. Now, as a potential car-buyer -- practicing how to buy a car could save you time and money!

For all first time car buyers, spending your time at understanding and learning car-buying principles can save you money. A skill you'll be proud to learn!

Planning the Purchase

Have your car-repair bills increased so high that buying a newer car is now necessary?

Does the family need a second car?

The personal needs of each consumer will direct which kind of car or truck is needed. Never buy a car to keep up with a friend or neighbor. Base your purchase on your needs not your wants in life!

Those needs should include:

1. Family size (number of members)

My family includes _____ members.

Also, do you transport others on a regular basis, which would increase your need?

2. Budget (both purchase and upkeep)

Remember, that a car costs a lot more than just a monthly payment -- assuming it is financed. Some people do save money to pay cash on a car. A budget outline follows, later.

3. Expected life of the car (its usage)

With greater car dependability, it is not unusual for many cars to go beyond 100,000 miles with good reliability.

The number of years you plan to use the car, before ex-changing it, must be accounted for in your future car purchases.

Often, many people fall in love with their cars and lose their perspective of what cars are really worth. A car's "true" value is measured by what others will pay for it, at the moment.

Never make a major car purchase on your first day of shopping for it!

Credit Reporting Agencies

Fully informed consumers are aware of their financial "standings" and credit profiles [We will outline some financial tracking tips, later on]. For your credit report, you only need to obtain a copy from the major reporting agencies. All are user friendly, and will provide basic instructions for interpretation of their reports:

Provide: Full name including initial, generation.
          Spouse's name; any maiden name.
          Current address with ZIP code, included.
          Previous address; going back five years.
          Social Security Number
          Year of birth and your signature.

Send to:

Experian (Free copy available, yearly.)
(formerly TRW Information services)
P.O. Box 8030
Layton, UT 84041-8030

Trans Union ($8.00)   EQUIFAX ($8.00)
National disclosure Ctr. Credit Info Service
P.O. Box 390   P.O. Box 740241
Springfield PA 19064   Atlanta GA 30374-0241

Parties to the Purchase

When going into buy a car, you need a good team; those around you who will help you make the best decisions, possible. Use your contacts to gather any and all the necessary car-buying information, before committing to a final car purchase:

1. Insurance Agents

Even if you pay cash for your car, it must be adequately insured. You must decide what's "adequate" for you and your family's protection, and not just what the minimum legal requirements might be.

Some cars require extra-high premiums to insure them. Your insurance agent can help you pre-select similar make and model cars with much lower premium requirements, if you ask them.

If you use the vehicle for business, or lease, your employer may require higher than normal levels of coverage.

2. Auto Dealers

When buying cars from used-car dealers, make sure they are legitimately licensed and have been doing business in the area for many years.

Talk to as many people as possible to get stories -- good or bad, about them.

3.   Auto Mechanics

In today's world, most families don't have a regular mechanic to service their cars. Instead, they use the dealer, or several local repair shops to service their car needs.

It is critical to know, in advance, what a car's true condition is before trying to purchase it. Having a regular mechanic to maintain your current cars with makes economical sense. For this mechanic can give you "another" opinion of the potential car purchase!

4. Financing Source

Pre-arrange your own car financing, always!

Exception: New-car-purchase loans having below market interest rates for extended periods of four years or more.

5. Department of Motor Vehicles (DMV)

For a small fee, the DMV will notify you who the car's previous owner is. Note: when you apply and pay their fee, though, they will notify the previous car-owner of your name and address, too, and the reason for DMV's releasing of this information.

6.   Financial Counselor

Money management assistance on a consulting basis is available to all consumers. Some consulting is low or not cost, and some consulting is provided at a high level of expertise and will cost money. Inquire, then decide what assistance you really need.

Financial Counseling

Complete financial counseling can involve estate planning, goal setting and legal interpretations of potential decisions.

Many people prefer to avoid the high costs of some professionals, and instead seek thrifty ways of obtaining help. One source is the non-profit Consumer Credit Counseling Service (CCCS), member services of the National Foundation for Consumer Credit (NFCC). there are 200 non-profit Services with over 1,200 counseling sites within the 50 United States, Canada and Puerto Rico, offering free or low cost, confidential counseling services. A local Service can be located by calling:

1-800-388-CCCS
(2227)

Some Services, such as Los angeles, have information available on-line:

www.wehelp@cccs.com

CCCS works to help consumers with financial awareness through general education, counseling on personal budgeting, the wise use of credit, and even planned debt liquidation. Each CCCS location provides professional counseling, in a confidential environment, to aid concerned consumers and rehabilitate financially distressed families regardless of race, sex, social position or financial status.
CCCS organizations are as much concerned with preventing financial problems as re-solving them for their clientele. CCCS's professional counselors examine ways to prevent future financial difficulties through budget or spending plans, in

addition to solving current financial problems for their clientele. Prevention can be accomplished by providing education to all age groups on how to use credit wisely through money management and other topic workshops in schools, businesses, and community organizations.

CCCS personnel are qualified professionals trained in the field of consumer credit. To insure continuing high standards, though, the NFCC requires every counselor at CCCS to complete a counselor certification program before working with their clientele.

Each non-profit "service-location" is managed, locally. Contact the CCCS nearest you, to see what services are available. Some of these services are:

1. **Counseling.** For budget, goal setting and money management. These services are offered face-to-face, or by mail/phone interviewing.

2. **Debt Management Programs.** For those unable to meet their contractual credit obligations, yet having some funds available, a program may be developed with the cooperation of creditors, to offer a more reasonable term of repayment.

3. **Housing Services.**
   (Housing cost is your largest budget item.)

    a. Pre-rental and Pre-Purchase
    b. Post Purchase Counseling
    c. Default Prevention Assistance
    d. Reverse Mortgage Counseling

4. **Education Workshop and Presentations.** Offered throughout the community, a variety of subjects are available on a scheduled or pre-arranged basis.

Car Insurance Requirements

Let your insurance company offer you information on cars and trucks they find best or worst, but from an insurance agent's perspective.

their information should include basic research data related to any car's survivability rates when in an accident, cost of repairs to the car-of choice and frequency of being stolen.

MAKE/MODEL/YEAR

Best5:_____

_____

_____

_____

_____

Worst5:_____

_____

_____

_____

_____

Financing-Option and Pre-approvals

Whether you are considering paying cash for your car or using out-side financing, you will not automatically get the best deal [lowest rates] based on any particular financing method.

Cash
Cash is king, but there is a greater temptation for a seller to turn your cash into his profit.

Credit Unions
If you have access to a credit union, you have good credit. Always start with your credit union when shopping for a car loan. They typically have the most favorable rates.

Banks
Sometimes, banks have car-loan drives, where they get extra low rates. Check your bank's car-loan rates when in the market for a car.

Dealer Arranged Loans
Worth exploring! Seasonally, manufacturer's offer extra low interest rates and extended loan periods to sell their product to the marketplace.

Finance Companies
Some consider this an avenue of near last resort. Their loan rates and fees will cost will always be higher.

The following chart will assist you in estimating a vehicle's payments when based on an estimate of the amount financed ($), at a given interest rate (%), and a term of repayments (number of months).

The factor represents the monthly payment per $1,000 of amount to be financed, for a given % rate.

Term of Repayment

Rate	24 mo. Factor	36 mo. Factor	48 mo. Factor
7%	$44.77	$30.88	$23.95
10%	$46.14	$2.27	$25.36
12%	$47.07	$33.21	$26.33
15%	$48.49	$34.67	$27.83
18%	$49.92	$36.15	$29.37

For example, if you wish to finance $9,000 for four years (48 months) at 10%, the factor is $25.36. Then multiply the factor ($25.36) times the "9" thousands to get (equals) $228.24 per month for four years of principle and interest on the total loan. In other words, 48 months of $228.24 equals $10,955.52 in total dollars paid by you at an interest rate of 10%. You will pay $1,955.52 to finance the total $9,000 loan.

Budget For the Used Car:

Car Payment $_____

Insurance (12 Months) $_____

License/Smog Fees $_____

Gas per Month $_____

Maintenance (Oil, tune-up costs) $_____

Repair Accrual (Ties, Transmission) $_____

Total Monthly Costs $_____
  (carry over to your total monthly budget figures)

Also, will you be considering any upgrades on the used car, once you have made the car purchase -- like a sound system, CD player, custom rims, alarm? If so, take potential costs into account.

217

Debt Obligations

Do not take on additional debt unless you have current obligations within reason and under financial control. As a rule of thumb, you should not have monthly payments in excess of 20% of your monthly net income. This would include all debts other than your rent or house payment. Add total to budget, now.

Type of debt	Balance Owed	Mo. Payment
Auto Loan	$_____	$_____
Student Loan	$_____	$_____
Personal Loan	$_____	$_____
Credit Cards	$_____	$_____
_____	$_____	$_____
_____	$_____	$_____
_____	$_____	$_____
_____	$_____	$_____
_____	$_____	$_____
Totals:	$_____	$_____

Budgeting the Purchase

TOTAL NET INCOME $_____

HOUSING $_____

FOOD $_____

INSURANCE $_____

MEDICAL $_____

SCHOOL/ CHILD CARE $_____

CLOTHING $_____

MISCELLANEOUS $_____

RECREATION $_____

SAVINGS/EMERGENCY $_____

DEBT PAYMENTS $_____

TOTAL EXPENSES (BEFORE CAR) $_____

TRANSPORTATION $_____
(Monthly Car Payment, Insurance, license, Gas, oil, Maintenance and Repairs)

TOTAL EXPENSES (AFTER CAR) $_____

Pricing Research (Available at most libraries)

Kelley Blue Book: Used car pricing book used by the auto industry and automobile auctions.

Edmund's Used Car Prices: Published several times a year, this book is for public consumption and not used by the auto industry as a pricing guide.

Consumer Reports Magazine: Their April issue -- used car ranking reports are useful information for serious car buyers wishing to select quality cars.

Kiplinger's Magazine: Their December issue has several excellent articles about choosing used-cars.

Car Shopping Phase Reminders:

1. Visit a minimum of five new car lots, before selecting used cars to negotiate for.

2. Shop during the week -- preferably early in the week.

3. Walk through the dealer's new car lot searching for inexperienced car salesmen to negotiate with.

4. Always remember the salesman's goal: to get you in any car and sell you today!

5. Always remember your goal: locate quality used car with excellent resell values in the future.

6. Get the salesman's business card, before leaving.

7. Test drive only the cars you are considering of buying, not the car the salesman "puts" you into.

8. Try to locate the previous owner, after you have completed your car-shopping phase. They may tell you a lot about the used car, before you try to make an offer for it at the dealers.

9. Never go into the salesman's office, during your car-shopping phase. Wait a few days before you return to negotiate for the car you really want.

Car-Lot information worth getting:

Vehicle: Make/Model/Year

Overall Appearance: Excellent/good/ Fair

Mileage -- (average is 12,000 miles per years)
Year _____   Mileage _____
Exterior: (never shop cars in the night time)

Paint _____   Lights _____
         Windows _____
Tires _____   Dents _____

Interior:

Dashboard   _____
Headliner   _____
Seats   _____
Electrical   _____
Trunk Area   _____
Under Hood Area   _____

Engine Sounds: (keep radio off) _____

Demonstration Drive: (15 minutes minimum)

Idle speed roughness   _____
Street speed   _____
Up hills & freeway   _____

Placed on a rack (undercarriage) Yes ___/No ___

A good mechanic will tell you if the car's condition
is free of major accidents, rust, or of suspicious
origin (new-welds in the middle of the car).

Trade-ins

Some consumers prefer to trade-in their old cars versus trying to resell them to private parties. If this is your intention, you should give the car a good cleaning and hold your ground to its worth:

a. Be sure the registration is current. If you own the car free and clear, do you have the title to it?

b. Has the oil been changed recently, and is the engine in good running order?

c. Was the car taken care of or does it look "tired" beyond its useful years?

d. Consider having the car detailed (under $100), if you feel the expense is justified:
   - Steam clean engine compartment
   - Wash, clean and wax the car
   - Vacuum and shampoo interior and trunk areas
   - Clean and protection for vinyl, plastic, and rubber surfaces of car

Pay-Off Figure

If a loan is outstanding on the car you plan to trade-in, obtain a current pay-off for 10 days and 30 days.

Car-Buying Phase: (Tips worth considering)

Never shop and buy on the same day. This is true for any major purchase you plan to make.

Knowledge is Power. Negotiate from an informed point of view when encountering car salesmen. Try to think like car salesmen do when buying a car. If you don't get your "fair" deal walk away, now!

Always take your spouse, family member or friend with you. Never go alone to buy a car, no exceptions!

Don't fall in "love" with any particular used-car. Cars are "consumable" items, there "true" cash value is in its resell worth -- to others, when resold.

Don't let the size of your monthly payment, bump-you-up to a more expensive car! Some car salesmen may say to you *"For $50 more we can get you into a luxury car you'll love, today."* If this happens to you, just leave car-lot, and do your shopping, elsewhere!

Time is money. Never rush into any deal salesmen offer you. Take your time and pre-plan your car-purchase, so the car-deal benefits you, mostly.

Warranty and Service Contracts

Most consumers are aware of new-car warranties, but usually fail to look closely at the dealer's limited used-car warranties. Ask lots of questions, until you are completely satisfied and understand the dealer's warranty. Service contracts cost a car buyer extra money and may be written into their contract. The price of the service is always negotiable. Dare to get the service for less -- even free! Be aware that less then 20% of the service contracts are ever used, which makes them very profitable items for dealers to sell. Their cost ranges from $300 to $1,500. Consider warranties and services contracts only when you can purchase them, for less.

Questions to Ask:

1. Is the service guarantee through the dealer or from an outside company?
2. Should the dealership go out of business, what protection remains for the buyer?

3. Review the repairs that are covered under the warranty.
4. What cost portion are you responsible for?
5. Must all repairs be done at the dealership?
6. What is the cancellation and refund policy?

Lemon Laws: Apply to new cars, mostly, but you should spend more time learning about cars shipped from out of state or if the car's license plates are missing or if the car's listed as Manufacturer's Buybacks (Lemons with excessive repairs done to them).

Payment Problems and Prevention

If you do finance you next car and then run into difficulty making your payments, contact with your lender is critical! Contact should be made, before the payment is due, not after. Different lending sources will handle your repayment problems, differently. Be prepared to explain and document your problem:

Would a due date change be enough to correct the problem? Could an extension of loan be arranged?

Prepare prior to contacting your lender:

1. Was the problem something beyond your control? Can you recover?
2. Keep all your documentation.
3. Was the auto loan given priority over unsecured debts such as credit cards?
4. Develop a plan of action:
   a. Review your current budget, carefully
   b. How much time will you need to recover?
   c. Should you sell or refinance?

Case Studies

Some individuals learn best by doing, or by example. Though most auto transaction don't involve damaging problems to the individual, here are some situations to be avoided, and likewise certain opportunities to cut a sharper deal with.

It can't be stressed enough, though, that doing you "homework" at your leisure, can save time, tempers and most of all your hard-earned money!

Here are a few cases histories out of the CCCS files. Again, though, most involve resolving problems for consumers, and it should not be assumed that all auto dealers and car salesmen are out to rip off consumers. Rather, their main motive for selling cars is to seek the greatest possible profits for their employers' and families.

Case Study # 1 (Avoid baiting from used to new)

John and Becky were newly weds, and he had shaky credit. Both work and hold good paying jobs. Unfortunately, their debt levels and living standards equaled their combined incomes.

They bought a used Toyota priced for $5,900. They had computed the payments at $278 for two years at 12%. They were talked into a new car for $280 per month at 9% interest, instead. They believed, upon signing the contract, their car loan was for only two years, even though their disclosure [contract] clearly showed four years and the financing of $11,250 -- nearly twice what they bargained for.

There is no right of recission (returning the car with no financial loss) in California. They couldn't give any information as to how they were misled, but admitted they didn't read the contract and other documents before signing them.

OUTCOME: The best CCCS could do was to streamline their budget. They showed the couple of their ability to pay $350/month and that they could pay off their car in 36 months.

Case Study # 2 (Insurability after purchase)

Mr. and Mrs. Jones (not their real names) had been living in Canada for the past two years. Upon returning to California, they sought to buy and finance a car. They put 20% down on the car which the dealer gladly accepted. Since the couple didn't have insurance to transfer on the purchased car, the dealer sold them a 30 day insurance binder. The contract stated that proper insurance must remain on the car for the term of the loan contract.

When the insurance binder expired, they still had not found a company to write a policy under $3,000 per year. They couldn't afford the policy's monthly payments of $250 on top on the car's $285 payment.

The lender, a finance company, added an insurance policy [of their own] to the Jones' car loan, adding $200 per month and increasing their payments to $485 per month. Though the insurance policy was less then the Jones' could find, the policy was only a vendor's single-interest policy which only gave protection to the car's financing! The policy had no liability/personal protection for the Jones.

OUTCOME: The car was repossessed with a deficiency of $3,800 including all the earned insurance credits.

Case Study # 3 (Come-on financing-rates and credit problems)

Jack was young, single and less than careful with his credit rating. Among other things, he had paid late fees on his previous car's loan, several times.

Responding to a newspaper-ad stating 5.9% interest, Jack visited the car dealership offering the ad. He signed for a 1993 Mitsubishi for $18,500 at $5.9%. With a 15% down payment (cash), the salesman said there would be not problems, so he drove the car home.

Three days later, the dealership's finance manager phoned Jack, saying the bank would not finance the car unless the contract was rewritten at 15% due to his less than good credit rating of the past. Jack argued that the dealership knew about his credit problems, before he signed. Even so, they continued to pressure him to return to the dealer.

OUTCOME: A counselor reviewed the situation and encouraged Jack to hold his ground. They should take the contract as is, or take the car back and give Jack a full refund. The dealer wanted to withhold $500 for the week Jack had the car, but finally the dealership arranged for the bank to accept it, as is.

Case Study # 4 (Warranty problems)

Bonnie co-signed a car-loan for her daughter to purchase a used Dodge car. The purchase included a service warranty for two years. Three weeks after the purchase, the car's engine "blew up." Upon examination, the dealership said a metal-piece fell into the engine and caused the damage, so it wasn't covered by their service warranty.

A counselor suggested that the daughter first get all this in writing. Then, to pay for a second "opinion" either by someone going to the dealership, or by having it towed to another location for examination. Bonnie paid $125 for a mobile mechanic to give his opinion.

OUTCOME: His finding didn't agree with the dealer's results. Because of this difference in opinions, arbitration was suggested. Through a third-party arbitrator, the dealership conceded the questionable cause of the engine failure and agreed to pay for all labor costs and 1/2 of the engine-parts. The client ended up paying $350 plus the $125 inspection fee, instead of the full $1,500 repair bill.

Case Study # 5 (Out-of-state title problems)

Commonly, dealerships take in trade-ins driven in from another state. William purchased such a used car -- Pontiac without license plates, and was informed the plates were personalized and returned.

Three months later, William was given a ticket for no plates. He went back to the dealership. They informed him that the company, holding title to the Pontiac was in New York, and that they refused to send back the car's title because the payoff figure was wrong and $800 was still owed on the car. Attempts had been made to find the seller of the car without any success.

William was informed that he would have to pay the difference due to get title to the Pontiac. He called the DMV Investigative Review Unit, but was having trouble getting a response from them. A call to DMV later showed their file was missing a response from the responsible dealership.

OUTCOME: With a threat of court, and a filing against the dealer's bond to do business, they finally paid the additional funds needed, and William secured title of the Pontiac in his name.

Case Study #6 (Buying into a salesman's confidence)

Sam, a church assistant, purchased a used Buick, after his "extensive" negotiating efforts. The salesman said he cut a "mean-deal" and "stole" the car from them. Six months later, facing layoff, Sam called his lender back. They encouraged him to return the car, so they could resell it.

Two months later, he received a notice saying he owed $4,500 on the repo he "stole" for $9,000. Going to the dealership, he asked for the facts on how this could have happened to him. They claimed the bank must have given his "car" away at some auction, therefore his problem was with the bank, not them.

OUTCOME: Upon investigation by CCCS professionals, Sam found that he had over paid $1,500 -- over full retail, and indeed, the bank resold the car for below wholesale. With CCCS help, Sam challenged the bank's role in the sale of his car. He got them to agree to their unattached follow-through at the auction, thus saving him $2,000. By cutting his loss to $2,500, Sam repaid the remaining balance over one year without any additional charges levied against him.

Case Study # 7 (Pre-approved Financing)

Sometimes, dealers play the numbers with their customers. In other words, they will take a chance selling their cars to customers who appears hard to get financed, because they believe several sources are available.

229

Mary had a new job. She was new in town and was living with a friend. She said her talk with the salesmen was all up-front and correct. She was assured (based on her application and credit report) of pre-approved credit up to $10,000. All this took place on a Saturday. Based on all this information, she selected a Fort Escort with low mileage on it. She had previous insurance and was aware of her good fortune -- knowing she got an excellent car deal.

Problems arose the following Tuesday, though, when she received a call from the finance manager at the dealership. He said she needed a co-signer for the loan to go through. She must produce a co-signer or face the loss of the Ford Escort.

OUTCOME: Based on CCCS advise, she involved the general manager who tried to undo the car-deal. Many have fallen for this "trap" and got their family members involved (unnecessary co-signing of contracts) when it was unnecessary.

Case Study # 8 (First car purchase experience)

Judith, living at home with her mother and planning her future independence bought a used BMW with a monthly payment of $350. One year later, her mother needed to relocate and Judith was forced to locate other living quarters. Without any real savings of he own, she needed a deposit, plus rental money to properly relocate.

Referred to one of our CCCS service centers, a counselor discovered her problem, quickly. Adding up her car-payment, insurance, registration, gas, and reasonable car care, she was spending about 58% of her net income for the BMW. With some $10,000 still owed on the car, her payments were going to be around for three more years.

She was encouraged to sell the BMW; but didn't understand how she ever got financing, anyway. It was explained that having no rent, utilities, etc. she had, on paper, a lot more to spend for a car. What was not considered was her future needs over the four-year term on the auto loan.

OUTCOME: Selling the car cost her $2,000, but cut the total living expenses down to allow her to move. This encouraged her mother to help further with the deposit and first month's rental.

Case Study # 9 (Overpricing trade-in values)

Philip had a worn out car to get rid of and was facing a long commute to the new job. He worked with a dealership to buy another car. He had only $1,500 cash down, though. The salesman showed a $3,000 trade-in value on a trade-in worth only $500-$1,000. The salesman was inflating the trade's value to get Philip financing.

When his first payment came due, he still didn't know who to make the payments to. He went to the dealer. He was told that the financing fell through at four different sources and that he must come up with addition cash to add to the down-payment. His contract said it was subject to lender approval.

Knowing the couldn't come up with more cash, and his payments would be hard to pay each month, he asked to return the car and get his trade and down-payment returned. The trade-in had been resold. Philip wanted to re-sign any documents. The car dealer, of course, didn't want to "unwind" the deal which showed them a $3,000 profit on the books.

OUTCOME: Dealer was forced to carry the contract.

What can you learn from these nine examples?

1. Don't base a purchase on a monthly car payment. Know the full terms, before signing any contract!

2. Know you are insured, before signing or taking delivery of any car.

3. Contract terms work to protect all parties. Don't give up any of your rights without questions, first!

4. Press for the facts in the deal, don't assume anyone is final-authority in negotiations.

5. Verify all documentation.

6. You must do your homework; don't depend solely on the word of others. Especially, if they have something to gain from the transaction.

7. The same goes for insurance, verify your financing before taking delivery of the car. If you have to wait a few days to see if the papers do go through okay.

8. Being a first time buyer is no excuse for being taken! Build your experience at buying cars over time.

9. Don't buy into any deceptive "inflating or deflating" scams some car salesmen use to sell cars.

✂ - - - - - - - - - - - - - - (Cut out) - - - - - - - - - - - - -

Make/Model/Year

1. _____

2. _____

3. _____

4. _____

5. _____

Make/Model/Year

1. _____

2. _____

3. _____

4. _____

5. _____

Shopping Cue Card

CAR-SHOPPING 'ET' LIST

A > location of dealer-car

B > the make/model/year

C > the car's mileage

D > the factory-option

E > the dealer's asking price

Get salesman's business card

Give dealer's car test drive

Does it look like a brand new?

TEST-DRIVE QUICK CHECK LIST

First impression of car _____

Exterior is free of dents _____

Interior: Seat not lumpy

look under floor mats _____

Wear on brake pedal _____

Armrest driver's side _____

Engine Compartment

everything is in place _____

No visable damage _____

Brakes work fine _____

Drives straight on road _____

No visable exhaust fume _____

Last impression of car _____

NEVER SHOP IN THE NIGHT   YES   NO

------ ✂ ------ (Cut out) ------

LOCATION **A** >   **E** >   Dealer Price: **K** >

CAR **B** >

Make/Model/Year

C > Mileage: **F** >   Dealer List:
                                Blue Book Value

D > Options: **G** >   Low:

                        H >   High:

(Physical data on back)   Buying Range:

                              I >   < **J**

Location/Physical Cue Card

CAR-SHOPPING 'ET' LIST

A > location of dealer-car

B > the make/model/year

C > the car's mileage

D > the factory-option

E > the dealer's asking price

Get salesman's business card

Give dealer's car test drive

Does it look like a brand new?

TEST-DRIVE QUICK CHECK LIST

First impression of car ___
Exterior is free of dents ___
Interior: Seat not lumpy ___
look under floor mats ___
Wear on brake pedal ___
Armrest driver's side ___
Engine Compartment
everything is in place ___
No visable damage ___

Brakes work fine ___
Drives straight on road ___
No visable exhaust fume ___
Last impression of car ___
YES   NO

NEVER SHOP IN THE NIGHT

LOCATION/PHYSICAL CUE CARD

-------------------(Cut out)-------------------

LOCATION A >   K >

CAR B >   E >   Dealer Price:

Make/Model/Year

C > Mileage: F >   Dealer List:
                           Blue Book Value

D > Options: G >   Low:

                     H >   High:

                           Buying Range:

(Physical data on back)   I >   < J

Location/Physical Cue Card

CAR-SHOPPING 'ET' LIST

A > location of dealer-car

B > the make/model/year

C > the car's mileage

D > the factory-option

E > the dealer's asking price

Get salesman's business card

Give dealer's car test drive

Does it look like a brand new?

TEST-DRIVE QUICK CHECK LIST

First impression of car ——

Exterior is free of dents ——

Interior: Seat not lumpy ——

look under floor mats ——

Wear on brake pedal ——

Armrest driver's side ——

Engine Compartment

everything is in place ——

No visable damage ——

Brakes work fine ——

Drives straight on road ——

No visable exhaust fume ——

Last impression of car YES NO

NEVER SHOP IN THE NIGHT

LOCATION/PHYSICAL CUE CARD

Trade: K >

Price of Car: I >

L > _____ Wholesale
Value only

Down: M >

Monthly: N >

Selling Room Cue Card

‐‐‐‐‐‐‐‐‐‐‐‐(Cut out)‐‐‐‐‐‐‐‐‐‐‐‐

Trade: K >

Price of Car: I >

L > _____ Wholesale
Value only

Down: M >

Monthly: N >

Selling Room Cue Card

APPENDIX A

Month-Payments Calculator

Within this appendix, you will find several monthly payment charts helpful in figuring approximate monthly payments. The charts are generated from a standard computer program. The number should be accurate enough to give you a rough idea of your monthly payments when you know the amount financed and interest rate.

For more accurate monthly-payment figures your credit union or bank will be glade to help you over the phone or in person.

DOLLARS	%	MONTHLY PAYMENTS			
		36	48	60	72 Mo.
10,000	10%	323	254	212	185
11,000	10%	355	279	234	204
12,000	10%	387	304	255	222
13,000	10%	419	330	276	241
14,000	10%	452	355	297	259
15,000	10%	484	380	319	278
16,000	10%	516	406	340	296
17,000	10%	549	431	361	315
18,000	10%	581	457	382	333
19,000	10%	613	482	404	352
20,000	10%	645	507	425	371
21,000	10%	678	533	446	389
22,000	10%	710	558	467	408
23,000	10%	742	583	489	426
24,000	10%	774	609	510	445
Dollars	%	36	48	60	72 Mo.

DOLLARS		MONTHLY PAYMENTS			
		36	48	60	72 Mo.
10,000	12%	332	263	222	196
11,000	12%	365	289	245	215
12,000	12%	399	316	267	235
13,000	12%	432	342	289	254
14,000	12%	465	368	311	274
15,000	12%	498	395	334	293
16,000	12%	531	421	356	313
17,000	12%	565	448	378	332
18,000	12%	598	474	400	352
19,000	12%	631	500	423	371
20,000	12%	664	527	445	391
21,000	12%	697	553	467	411
22,000	12%	731	579	489	430
23,000	12%	764	606	512	450
24,000	12%	797	632	534	469
DOLLARS	%	36	48	60	72 Mo.

DOLLARS	%	MONTHLY PAYMENTS			
		36	48	60	72 Mo.
10,000	14%	342	273	233	206
11,000	14%	376	301	256	229
12,000	14%	410	328	279	247
13,000	14%	444	355	302	268
14,000	14%	478	383	326	288
15,000	14%	513	410	349	309
16,000	14%	547	437	372	330
17,000	14%	581	465	396	350
18,000	14%	615	492	419	371
19,000	14%	649	519	442	392
20,000	14%	684	547	465	412
21,000	14%	718	574	489	433
22,000	14%	752	601	512	453
23,000	14%	786	601	512	474
24,000	14%	820	656	558	495
DOLLARS	%	36	48	60	72 Mo.

DOLLARS	%	MONTHLY PAYMENTS			
		36	48	60	72 Mo.
10,000	16%	352	283	243	217
11,000	16%	387	312	267	239
12,000	16%	422	340	292	260
13,000	16%	457	368	316	232
14,000	16%	492	397	340	304
15,000	16%	527	425	365	325
16,000	16%	563	453	389	347
17,000	16%	598	482	413	369
18,000	16%	633	510	438	390
19,000	16%	668	538	462	412
20,000	16%	703	567	486	434
21,000	16%	738	595	511	456
22,000	16%	773	623	535	477
23,000	16%	808	652	559	499
24,000	16%	844	680	584	521
DOLLARS	%	.36	48	60	72 Mo.

DOLLARS	%	MONTHLY PAYMENTS			
		36	48	60	72 Mo.
10,000	18%	362	294	254	228
11,000	18%	398	323	279	251
12,000	18%	434	353	305	297
13,000	18%	470	382	330	297
14,000	18%	506	411	356	319
15,000	18%	542	441	381	342
16,000	18%	578	470	406	365
17,000	18%	615	499	432	388
18,000	18%	651	529	457	411
19,000	18%	687	558	482	443
20,000	18%	723	587	508	456
21,000	18%	759	617	533	479
22,000	18%	795	646	559	502
23,000	18%	832	676	584	525
24,000	18%	868	705	601	547
DOLLARS	%	36	48	60	72 Mo.

Appendix B

INSPECTING YOUR PURCHASE
SIX WAYS TO RECOGNIZE A LEMON!
Copyright 1991 - Don Massey

You have found a car you may want to buy. The salesman
has answered all the questions to your satisfaction. The
price is negotiable. Now comes the fun: inspection of the
vehicle! Take your time and enjoy it.

Don't hurry the inspection. Let the salesman know you
are picky! This attitude will help you negotiate a better
deal. As you look over the car, verbalize all the problems
you find. Your job is to convince him the car is not worth
what he thinks. In fact, you want to create the impression
your doing him a favor buying such a car. Be subtle! Don't
actually say what I just wrote. By pointing out all the
problems with the car you'll be accomplishing the same
thing.

Make a list of the defects as you inspect. You can use
this list as a bargaining tool when you begin to negotiate
the price. Every problem you AND he are aware takes
dollars off his asking price.

There are some basic tools you should take to help do a good inspection. A flashlight: use it to look for rust in wheel wells. Have some rags to wipe your hands and to check fluid levels. A magnet will help you determine if plastic body filler has been used to replace rusted metal. Don't rely on your memory. A small note pad and pen should be used to keep track of the defects you find.

There are six parts to a thorough car inspection.
1. EYEBALLS
2. MILEAGE
3. EXTERIOR
4. INTERIOR
5. ENGINE/DRIVE TRAIN
6. TEST DRIVE

EYEBALLS

What is your first eyeball impression of the car? If it looks good, it must be good!. Right? Wrong, wrong, wrong! This is the common mistake of most car buyers. They buy a car based on looks. Dealers know this and have "detail men" who are experts in making a car look good.. It is their job to make a car look as appealing as possible. They wash it, clean the engine, touch-up the paint, shampoo the upholstery and carpet, make minor repairs, add tire dressing, repaint engine parts and dress the wiring under the hood. They do their darndest to make you think, "Wow! This car is really a nice, clean car". It is clean but how "nice" demands a closer look. By doing a good inspection you minimize your chances of getting a lemon.

Remember, the dealer sells you the car as-is. The only reason he will consider repairing the problems you discover after the sale is for good-will. What you see is what you get and that leads us right into the inspection.

MILEAGE

The mileage of a vehicle can be used as a general indicator for common problems. You'll want to look for these problems when you do your inspection. History has shown that after major milestones certain parts may fail.

A car should average 12,000 miles a year. Anything substantially more or less can mean a problem. When a car reaches 100,000 or more miles, the need for a thorough inspection is nil. If you do buy a car with this kind of mileage, make sure you steal it i.e., 300 to 500 dollars. It is very risky to buy this kind of car.

So let's look at the things to watch for at major mileage milestones.

LESS THAN 20,000 MILES

A car with this few miles has either no problems or a lot of problems. Be careful, it could be a lemon! It may have had the odometer rolled back. But buyer, you beware! Ask the dealer who was the previous owner. If possible contact the owner to ask why they sold or trader a low mileage car. You may discover the odometer has been turned back.

20,000 to 30,000 MILES

Brakes and tires may be going at this mileage. Check them. Look for unusual wear of the tires. Starters, alternators and electrical operated systems may begin failing.

30,000 to 40,000 MILES

The suspension system is beginning to weaken in this middle mileage car. Use the road test to check it. Does it shimmy or pull to one side? Listen for transmission noise and clunk in the universal joints when starting up or shifting gears. When was the last front end alignment done? Check the tires for abnormal wear indicating a suspension problem.

40,000 to 50,000 MILES

Transmissions, wheel bearings, universal joints, belts, hoses, brakes, tires and power options are potentially in trouble. Accelerate the engine. Look for smoke. Black smokes means a tune-up or valve job. Blue smoke means oil is being burned in the cylinders. Don't buy the car.

50,000 MILES AND MORE

Check all the previous items carefully. Pay particular attention to oil burning and any transmission or universal joint noise.

MILEAGE CONSIDERATIONS

What's a high mileage car. You should not just consider the miles on the odometer but how long do you plan to keep the car and how many miles a year do you drive. Example: The car you're looking at has 65,000 miles. The salesman keeps stressing the low mileage. But you know you'll finance the car for three years and drive 20,000 miles a year back and forth to work. You'll have over 100,000 miles on the car and still owe a year's payments. You pass on this one. Too much of a chance in the last year of big repair bills. You need one with 35,000 miles or less.

EXTERIOR

Walk around the car. Never, never, never inspect a car at night or under artificial lights. A beauty at night under soft lights can become a dog the next day in the bright sunlight.
One of the things the outside inspection will show is if the car has been in an accident. Another is the presence of rust; obvious or hidden.

Here is a 10 point inspection list:

GLASS

Is the glass broken or cracked? Does the car have a current vehicle inspection?

LIGHTS

Try all the lights, including brake and turn signals. Do the turn signals self-cancel after turning?

RUST

Inspect carefully. Use your small magnet. Check rocker panels, wheel wells, fenders and doors for plastic filler. Filler will be hiding rust that will pop out later! Get down and look under the car. See any rust? Look for weld marks on the frame because of major accident damage. While your down there, look for fluid leaks on the car and on the ground.

Don't buy a car with rust problems. Car dealers call rust "cancer". It's deadly!

PAINT

Check to see if the car is repainted. You can tell by lifting the molding edge on the windshield right at the paint line. Also there may be paint over-spray in the engine compartment or on the fire-wall. A new paint job may be hiding accident repair damage or rust! Watch out for it! If you find no problems, the new paint job is a big plus! If the paint is only faded, a detail shop can buff it out to a like-new look.

Look for blisters in the paint on the rocker panels, on the bottoms of the doors and around the door and window frames. These are usually severe rust problems surfacing under the paint. Sometimes you can pop these blisters with a finger nail.

DOOR, HOOD and TRUNK

Do they all work? Do they all lock? Are they all in alignment with the body? Open each door and gently push it shut. Don't slam it. If it hits and bounces off the latch, it is mis-aligned. This could mean frame damage. Be alert for frame welds when checking under the car. Look in the trunk. Check under the mat for rust. Are there a spare tire, lug wrench and jack? Is the spare tire the right size for the car. Is it flat? Does the lug wrench fit the lugs? While your at the rear of car, check for signs of a trailer hitch, actual or removed. Towing heavy loads can devastate an engine and transmission.

TAIL PIPE

Check the deposit on the inside with your finger. It should be a white or grey residue. Black and sooty may mean a tune-up. Black and gummy means the car is burning oil! Is the muffler and catalytic converter intact?

TIRES

Are they ok? Do they show any abnormal wear because of suspension or alignment problems?

SHOCKS

Bounce each corner up and down 4 or 5 times. The car should only bounce once after you stop. Check to see if any of the shocks are leaking.

ALIGNMENT

Park the car on a flat level surface. Move away about 30 feet from the car. Check the car. Does it set level? Squat down and look. Are the tires in line with each other?

WHEELS

Grab hold of the top of the front wheels. Try to pull and push them to see if they wobble. Wheel bearings or ball joints may be bad if they do.

GAS TANK

If the car uses unleaded fuel only, is the retainer for the smaller pump nozzles still in the filler pipe? Some owners punch them out to use cheaper leaded gasoline. This destroys the catalytic converter and the car will fail state inspection.

INTERIOR

The inside inspection of the car may give you clues on how well the car was taken care of. If the interior was neglected, the owner probably treated the mechanical needs the same. A car that has been maintained is worth more.

Here is a 7 point inspection list for the interior:

SEATS

Set in each one. Are they lumpy or have broken springs? Any tears or rips? Is the back seat worn (Taxicab)? Do they slide back and forth easily?

MATS

Look under the mats and carpets for rust. Do the pedals reflect equivalent wear for the mileage on the odometer?

DOORS

Look for abnormal wear on the driver's armrest. Does the wear match the odometer miles?

SMELL

Is it musty smelling or strongly deodorized to cover smells? Musty smells can mean leaks and rust or worse, a car that has been flooded. Dealer's use deodorants in their used cars so it's not easy to "smell a rat" on a dealer's lot.

ODOMETER

What is the mileage? Does it meet your standards for the age of the vehicle? If it is high mileage, were they highway or city miles? Highway miles are half the wear and tear of stop and go city travel.

In 1989, a federal law requires the odometer reading be entered on the title in all states. In 1972, a federal law made it illegal to change, disconnect or tamper with the odometer. It still happens, however, so check the dashboard for scratch marks, missing screws or other indications. Are all the numbers on the odometer lined up? Rolling back the odometer sometimes causes misaligned numbers.

Dealer's won't role back the odometer because of fear of losing their license. Wholesalers who sell to dealers have been known to do this and then "fix" the title to show the lower mileage.

INSTRUMENT PANEL

Do all the gauges, lights and controls work? Horn? Radio? Air conditioning? Heater? Do all the idiot lights come on when you turn the key? If not, they may be disconnected to cover up a problem. Do they go out when you start the engine? Is it a rat's nest under the dashboard? Any loose or hanging wiring? Why?

WINDOWS
Do they ALL operate smoothly?

ENGINE/TRANSMISSION

RADIATOR
Look into the radiator. Is there an oil film on top of the water? If there is, it indicates oil is leaking into the cooling system. This means a cracked block. If the water is rusty, the radiator may need replacing soon. Check inside the filler neck with your finger. Sludge or gunk means a "stop-leak" has been used to plug holes in the system.

OIL
Oil that is murky brown, grey or bubbly has water in it. A sure indication of a cracked block. Grit or gum in the oil means it hasn't been changed often. A dealer usually has the oil changed so this may be a tough one to spot.

TRANSMISSION FLUID
Check it. Low means there is a leak. Should be a red color. Brown means there has been no maintenance done on the transmission. Smell the fluid. If it smells burned, it means the transmission has lots of wear. Pieces of metal in the fluid show the gears are being ground off. Stay away from any transmission problems.

ENGINE
Check for oil leaks. If the engine has been cleaned, you won't see any oil leaks. If so, extend your test drive to 30-45 minutes with some high speed highway driving. Look for leaks again after the test drive.

Are the pollution control devices intact? Some areas of the country (California) require the seller to provide a smog certificate. Check and understand your state laws regarding air quality control devices in the sale and purchase of cars. Make sure the dealer follows the regulations If the devices are not present, you may be in for several hundreds of dollars in repairs before you can sell the car or have it pass the next inspection!

BELTS

Are the belts frayed, cracked or loose? Squeeze the water hoses. Are they soft and supple or hardened and cracked? Check for excess play with the fan blade which means the water pump drive shaft may be ready to fail.

TEST DRIVE

Now it's time to see how the car "feels". Start the engine. Get out. Open the hood. Listen to the engine. Check out any unusual noises. Did the car start easily? Does it idle smoothly. Be concerned about a rough idle. It could mean anything from a simple tune-up to a major engine overhaul.

Drive the car on a variety of road conditions. This should include a bumpy road, freeway driving, city driving and hills. Drive the car with the window down. Don't let the salesman turn on the radio. This is a common way to cover any "odd" noises you might hear. You want to "hear" the car.

The following 7 point checklist will help you decide on the car.

STEERING

Look out the window. Does the tire turn at the same time you turn the steering wheel? If it doesn't turn in the first 2 inches of steering wheel movement, you may have major suspension problems. On power steering, turn and lock the wheels in both directions. There should be no screeches or bouncing.

EXHAUST

As your driving, check the exhaust in the rear view mirror. Blue smoke means burning oil. Don't buy! Black smoke means it may need a tune up. White smoke when starting is only water vapor in the exhaust pipe. White smoke during driving means water in the cylinders!

BRAKES

Check to see if there is at least 2 inches between the pedal and floor when you push it down as far as you can. Do the brakes screech, pull or fade when applied? Make a quick stop. Does the car pull or dip to one side? If it does, it could mean brake and/or suspension trouble.

Check the parking brake on a hill. Does it hold? If not the rear brakes may be worn out or the hand brake needs adjusting.

♠

ALIGNMENT

Does the car track straight when you let go of the wheel?

ENGINE

Any unusual noises? Pinging or tapping? Does it idle smoothly? Was it easy to start? Any acceleration hesitation? If there appears to be engine problems, don't buy until you have a mechanic check it out.

TRANSMISSION

Move the transmission from drive to reverse with your foot on the brake. You should hear nothing or a soft thump. A clunk means problems. Don't buy! Drive the car in reverse for at least 200 feet to check its operation. The transmission should shift smoothly and operate with no noise. Does it balk or jerk during shifting? If it does, don't buy the car.

LEAKS

Put the car through a self service car wash to check for water leaks.

TIME

Drive the car for at least 10 - 15 miles (45 minutes). At the end of the test drive, leave the engine running, raise the hood and check the engine compartment again. Look, listen and smell for anything unusual or different: noise, smoke, oil leaks, burning smell, squeaks, pinging, any problems? If so, investigate.

LOOKING UNDERNEATH

After the test drive, TELL the salesman you want to put it on their lift to look underneath. Looking at the bottom will give you a different prospective about the car. Check the following.

Engine/transmission leaks
Brake line leaks
Shock absorber leaks
Accident damage repair
Check fender wells for creases or repairs
Frame welds
Rocker panel rust

A FINAL COMMENT

If after your inspection, you feel uncomfortable about the car, ask to take it to your mechanic for a thorough check. Reputable dealers will allow this. If the salesman seems to be hesitant, you'll need to walk away from this one. Don't buy from the dealer who is not willing to let you protect your interests in the deal. Remember, you buy as-is. No guarantees or returns.

Appendix C

GETTING YOUR CAR READY FOR SALE
Copyright 1991 - Don Massey

How your car looks will make a big difference in how fast your car sells. By spending a few hours and a little elbow grease you will also increase your profit.

The first impression the potential buyer has of your vehicle is the most important part of the sale. People do buy by looks. The way a car looks affects the judgment of the buyer. It can create either a positive or negative image.

A clean car gives the impression the car was well cared for. We all know this is not true, but the emotions created by a spic-and-span automobile will over-rule the logic of the typical buyer. Car dealers have always known this and usually have their own in-house detail men.

You have two ways to prepare your car. The first is to let someone else do it. A detail shop can do a great job with little hassle for you. You'll get your car back in tip-top sparkling condition. The second is to do the work yourself. The following checklist will help you do a great job.

WASHING AND WAXING

Clean the car thoroughly. Take time to clean out all the cracks and crevices. A toothbrush can work wonders around chrome and moldings. Take the car to a self service high pressure wash and clean in the wheel wells and the under carriage of the car. If you really do a thorough job, this will take 2-3 hours! Try to get it as spotless as the day it came off the showroom floor.

After this, apply the best wax you can afford. Don't spare a couple of extra bucks for a cheaper wax.

Don't forget to thoroughly clean the tires and wheel covers. Put tire dressing on after the cleaning.

TOUCH-UP

As your washing, you'll find all the paint dings and scratches that need to be fixed. A small tube or bottle of touch-up paint can be purchased at your auto parts store. Do the touch-up before you wax the car. Paint does not stick well to a waxed surface.

If the paint is really faded, you might consider an inexpensive paint job at a local paint shop.

INTERIOR

The interior must be cleaned thoroughly. Shampoo the carpet and upholstery. Completely wash and clean the interior. Again a toothbrush will work wonders in cleaning the dirt and dust out of the cracks and crannies in the dash and on the doors. Don't forget to clean the glove compartment and trunk. After your done, buy some "new car" deodorant to make it smell like new.

Replace the floor mats if they are worn. Do a detail check of the interior for tears, breaks and missing items. Fix them.

Now test these items to make sure they work.

Air conditioner
Antenna
Backup lights
Cigarette lighter

Clock
Defroster
Doors
Emergency flashers
Heater
Horn
Lights
Locks
Mirror's
Radio/Tape deck
Tachometer
Tilt wheel
Stop lights
Turn Signals
Windshield wiper
Windshield washer

Also check all the lights. Don't forget easily forgotten ones like the dome, license plate and the glove compartment light.

THE ENGINE COMPARTMENT

Have the engine steam cleaned. If you need too save money, buy a couple of cans of engine degreaser and clean the engine at a self service car wash. If the engine was oil covered, find the source of the oil and correct it.

After the engine is clean, do a visual check. Are there any loose wires or broken items? Now check the hoses and belts. Clean the battery terminals.

Change the oil and coolant. Don't forget the automatic transmission fluid. Check it and the battery, and brake fluid. Replace the air filter.

MISCELLANEOUS

Check and correct rattles and squeaks. Oil door, hood and trunk hinges.

Have all the documents ready: a current title, registration papers, warranties, service records and owner's manual. Leave them in the glove compartment so you'll have them easily available.

The CAR BUYER'S GUIDE

How to Beat the Salesman at His Own Game

STERLING AWARD

"Car Salesmen dread a buyer who's ready."
L.A. TIMES

Based on The Car Buyer's Art by:

DARRELL PARRISH

THE CAR BUYER'S GUIDE

(VHS VIDEO ONLY)

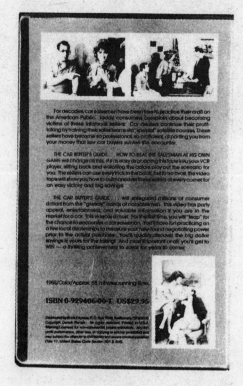

The SPREAD-THE-WORD offer is extended to all. Any four book order, or combination of, will receive free of charge THE CAR BUYER'S GUIDE video! Loan your books out to your friends and associates. They will return your books and tell you many "victory" stories over the infamous seller--THE CAR SALESMAN! Thank you and happy hunting!

The
CAR
BUYER'S
ART

How to Beat the Salesman at His Own Game

"Car Salesmen
dread a buyer
who's ready."
L.A. TIMES

DARRELL PARRISH

THE CAR BUYER'S ART

Now that you are a pro at new-car buying, how about helping your friends and associates save money, too! Your friends and associates value their money and will thank you over and over for "lending" them one of your copies of THE CAR BUYER'S ART.

Book Express extends a special "spread-the-work" offer to concerned individuals wishing to help their friends and associates win at the car-buying "game." A "game" car salesmen have specially devised for taking extra cash from the unwary consumers in the marketplace. Book Express is now offering a free one-hour [VHS] video called, THE CAR BUYER'S GUIDE to individuals who purchase four copies or combination of four titles: THE CAR BUYER'S ART, USED CARS and LEASE CARS.

This special video/books offer retails at $50.00 plus, and is now yours for $25.00, plus $4.00 shipping/handling. Save your friends and associates a bundle of car-buying/leasing dollars by taking advantage of this "spread-the-word" offer, today!

SEND CHECK OR MONEY ORDER TO:

BOOK EXPRESS
P.O. BOX 1249
BELLFLOWER CA 90706

Name:_____

Address:_____

City:_____

State: _____ ZIP:_____

LEASE CARS

How to Get One

From the author of
THE CAR BUYER'S ART

DARRELL PARRISH

LEASE CARS... How To Get One

Now that you are a pro at new-car leasing, how about helping your friends and associates save money, too! Your friends and associates value their money and will thank you over and over for "lending" them one of your copies of LEASE CARS.

Book Express extends a special "spread-the-work" offer to concerned individuals wishing to help their friends and associates win at the car-leasing "game." A "game" car salesmen have specially devised for taking extra cash from the unwary consumers in the marketplace. Book Express is now offering a free one-hour [VHS] video called, THE CAR BUYER'S GUIDE to individuals who purchase four copies or combination of four titles: THE CAR BUYER'S ART, USED CARS and LEASE CARS.

This special video/books offer retails at $50.00 plus and is now yours for $25.00, plus $4.00 shipping/handling. Save your friends and associates a bundle of car-buying/leasing dollars by taking advantage of this "spread-the-word" offer, today!

SEND CHECK OR MONEY ORDER TO:

BOOK EXPRESS
P.O. BOX 1249
BELLFLOWER CA 90706

Name:_____

Address:_____

City:_____

State: _____ ZIP:_____

USED CARS

How to Buy One

From the author of
THE CAR BUYER'S ART

DARRELL PARRISH

USED CARS...How To Buy One

Now that you are a pro at used-car buying, how about helping your friends and associates save money, too! Your friends and associates value their money and will thank you over and over for "lending" them one of your copies of USED CARS.

Book Express extends a special "spread-the-work" offer to concerned individuals wishing to help their friends and associates win at the car-buying "game." A "game" car salesmen have specially devised for taking extra cash from the unwary consumers in the marketplace. Book Express is now offering a free one-hour [VHS] video called, THE CAR BUYER'S GUIDE to individuals who purchase four copies or combination of four titles: THE CAR BUYER'S ART, USED CARS AND LEASE CARS.

This special video/books offer retails at $50.00 plus and is now yours for $25.00, plus $4.00 shipping/handling. Save your friends and associates a bundle of car-buying/leasing dollars by taking advantage of this "spread-the-word" offer, today!

SEND CHECK OR MONEY ORDER TO:

BOOK EXPRESS
P.O. BOX 1249
BELLFLOWER CA 90706

Name:_____

Address:_____

City:_____

State: _____ ZIP:_____

"$4,000 Profit, First 2 Months"

"Thanks, It really works!"...

...says C.M. of Elkhart, IN

HERE'S HOW!

Every year Americans buy and sell more than 15 million used cars. Over 50% of these sales are by individuals.

People, just like you, are in the business of quietly buying and selling cars...from home. One at a time. They pocket hundreds in profits on every deal. Now, You will, too!

They know the secrets of how to buy good cars at below wholesale prices (no fixer-uppers). Then they advertise in small newspaper classifieds, selling as individuals...with hundreds of dollars of profit on each sale! Now, You will, too!

IT'S SIMPLE!

You have probably sold a car in the newspaper classifieds. Remember how easy it was? You placed an ad. People called. They looked. They made an offer. You agreed and they drove away in their "new" car. Now do the same thing weekly and make thousands!

> *Discover all of the details of this fantastic, little-known business in my new edition of "USED CAR GOLD MINE". It's crammed full of insider's secrets and the result of years of experience and know-how.*

ANYONE CAN DO IT!

If you like cars, then this is really for you! Men and women can make this profitable plan work, full or part-time. You'll learn by doing! You don't need mechanical skills. You won't be a salesman. The cars you'll buy will sell themselves!

Let me introduce myself. My name is Don Massey. I've been in business more than 20 years. I've enjoyed working and counseling with hundreds of folks, just like you.

As a hobby, I research, write and give seminars about little-known, but highly profitable businesses. Thousands have bought my books and attended my seminars. But enough about me.

I want YOU to be successful with this new plan.

GET RID OF YOUR MONEY WORRIES FOR GOOD!

You'll buy cars under book value. Then turn around and easily resell them at maximum profits, in your spare time...at home! These fast sellers will make you as much as: $500 to $1000 each. Take a second to think what you could do with the monthly income of selling one a week!

Please accept this invitation to make $1000's in your spare time! Take the first step **NOW...** **ORDER TODAY!**

BOOK ORDERS

Thank you for your special interest in winning at the car buying/leasing "game." The "con-game" car salesmen have devised! We think the rest of your car buying/leasing experiences with car salesmen should prove both rewarding and economical to you.

Since, you have read one or more of our books. It makes good sense to help your friends and relatives save money with one of our car-buying/leasing titles. Any book that can help readers save thousands of car-buying dollars is a great gift item. Many past readers have already reported their car buying/leasing "victories" to us, in letter form! In fact, some of their "buying-strategies" have been placed inside Mr. Parrish's recent book revisions to help us all win in the automobile marketplace.

For single or multiple book purchases of: Car buyer's Art, Used Cars, and Lease Cars, Book Express will ship your book order, quickly. The book prices and shipping cost [$1.50 fee applies to the total book/books order] are listed on the reverse side. Please, indicate your mailing address, clearly, so Book Express' personnel can ship your order to the correct location. Thank you for your order.

BOOK EXPRESS

PS. For credit card purchasers of the above book titles:

Telephone: 1 800 ALL BOOK, anywhere in the USA!

BOOK ORDER FORM

Please rush my book order. My check/money order is enclosed with this book-order form. I have indicated which book or books are of interest to me and have included the $1.50 S & H charge to assist in your shipping and handling costs for processing my order. Also, my address is printed clearly to avoid mailing delays. Please process my order, quickly! Thank you.

****MENU****

[ONLY CURRENT EDITIONS WILL BE SHIPPED]

_____ copies - USED CARS 2nd Edition ----- $5.95
_____ USED CARS 3rd Ed. [Available Apr 1997] ---- $9.95
_____ copies - LEASE CARS 2nd Ed. -------- $6.95
_____ LEASE CARS 3rd Ed. [Available Aug 1997] --- $9.95
_____ copies - CAR BUYER'S ART 5th Ed. -- $6.95
_____ CAR BUYER'S ART 6th Ed. [Avail. Aug 1998] -- $9.95

BOOK ORDER AMOUNT DUE   _____

Please add $1.50 S & H fee $1.50 (per order)

T O T A L   A M O U N T   DUE

_____

SEND CHECK OR MONEY ORDER TO:

BOOK EXPRESS
P.O. BOX 1249
BELLFLOWER CA 90706

Name:_____

Address:_____

City:_____

BOOK ORDERS

Thank you for your special interest in winning at the car buying/leasing "game." The "con-game" car salesmen have devised! We think the rest of your car buying/leasing experiences with car salesmen should prove both rewarding and economical to you.

Since, you have read one or more of our books. It makes good sense to help your friends and relatives save money with one of our car-buying/leasing titles. Any book that can help readers save thousands of car-buying dollars is a great gift item. Many past readers have already reported their car buying/leasing "victories" to us, in letter form! In fact, some of their "buying-strategies" have been placed inside Mr. Parrish's recent book revisions to help us all win in the automobile marketplace.

For single or multiple book purchases of: Car buyer's Art, Used Cars, and Lease Cars, Book Express will ship your book order, quickly. The book prices and shipping cost [$1.50 fee applies to the total book/books order] are listed on the reverse side. Please, indicate your mailing address, clearly, so Book Express' personnel can ship your order to the correct location. Thank you for your order.

BOOK EXPRESS

PS. For credit card purchasers of the above book titles:

Telephone: 1 800 ALL BOOK, anywhere in the USA!

BOOK ORDER FORM

Please rush my book order. My check/money order is enclosed with this book-order form. I have indicated which book or books are of interest to me and have included the $1.50 S & H charge to assist in your shipping and handling costs for processing my order. Also, my address is printed clearly to avoid mailing delays. Please process my order, quickly! Thank you.

****MENU****

[ONLY CURRENT EDITIONS WILL BE SHIPPED]

_____ copies - USED CARS 2nd Edition ----- $5.95
_____ USED CARS 3rd Ed. [Available Apr 1997] ---- $9.95
_____ copies - LEASE CARS 2nd Ed. -------- $6.95
_____ LEASE CARS 3rd Ed. [Available Aug 1997] --- $9.95
_____ copies - CAR BUYER'S ART 5th Ed. -- $6.95
_____ CAR BUYER'S ART 6th Ed. [Avail. Aug 1998] -- $9.95

BOOK ORDER AMOUNT DUE   _____

Please add $1.50 S & H fee $1.50 (per order)

T O T A L   A M O U N T   DUE

_____

SEND CHECK OR MONEY ORDER TO:

BOOK EXPRESS
P.O. BOX 1249
BELLFLOWER CA 90706

Name:_____

Address:_____

City:_____